FAMILYLIFE presents
weekend to remember
love like you mean it

name Audrey Roe (Pork) .... conference date ....

take it home

things to remember or apply:

○ ....
○ ....
○ ....
○ ....
○ ....
○ ....

my top three priorities:

○ ....
  ....

○ ....
  ....

○ ....
  ....

Published by FamilyLife

© 1985 Campus Crusade for Christ
First edition 1985

© 2007, 2008 FamilyLife
Second edition 2007, Third edition, 2008

Printed in China
ISBN: 978-1-60200-121-3

14 13 12 11 10 09 08   1 2 3 4 5 6 7 8

FamilyLife owes a debt of gratitude to a special couple whose lives and material helped shape this ministry from its inception. Don and Sally Meredith, president and cofounders respectively of Christian Family Life, Inc., and authors of Two Becoming One, *not only gave this ministry a great start, but also an invaluable message for marriage today.*

FAMILYLIFE

Help for today. Hope for tomorrow.

Dennis Rainey, President
5800 Ranch Drive
Little Rock, Arkansas 72223
1.800.FL.TODAY ● FamilyLife.com

A ministry of Campus Crusade for Christ, Inc.

time	topic		page	guest
	introduction/FamilyLife information		1-9	
7:00-7:30	welcome to your weekend to remember			all
7:30-8:30	why marriages fail		11	all
8:30-8:45	break (resource center open)			all
8:45-9:30	can we talk?		23	all
9:30-9:50	project (resource center open)		30	all

friday

time	topic		page	guest
8:00-8:30	resource center open			
8:30-9:20	unlocking the mystery of marriage		35	all
9:20-9:35	break (resource center open)			all
9:35-10:25	from how to wow		45	all
10:25-11:40	project (resource center open)		53/56	married
	so you wanna get married	pre-married manual	5	pre-married
11:40-12:30	what every marriage needs		61	all
12:30-2:00	lunch (resource center open)			all
2:00-3:05	we fight too		83	all
3:05-3:35	HomeBuilders project		93	all
3:35-3:50	break (resource center open)			
3:50-4:45	marriage after dark		99	all
	project (complete before Sunday sessions)		106/112	all
4:45-5:45	two becoming one	pre-married manual	35	pre-married
	resource center open until 5:30 p.m.			
sat. evening	date night			

saturday

time	topic	page	guest
8:15-8:45	staff opportunities meeting (room to be announced)	optional	
9:00-10:30	woman to woman	119	all women
	man to man	137	all men
10:30-11:15	make it personal project (resource center open)	135/148	all
11:15-12:00	how marriages thrive	151	all
12:00-12:30	leaving a legacy	157	all
	appendices	163	
	resource center open 20 minutes after last session		

sunday

welcome to the
weekend to remember

Dennis and Barbara Rainey

We're glad you're here. No doubt you have overcome obstacles to arrive here with us. You carved time out of a busy schedule, arranged time off from work, and saved funds for registration and hotel costs. Now sit back, relax, and focus on your relationship with the most important person on earth—your spouse.

What you're about to hear this weekend is not just one couple's opinion on marriage. It is the result of more than three decades of biblical research by a team of men and women who distilled what it takes to have a successful marriage and family. You'll learn about timeless blueprints for marriage, about commitment and communication, and about romance and resolving conflict.

To make the most of your weekend, we encourage you to do four things:

- Listen carefully during the messages to the overall purpose and plan for marriage, even if you're not sure you agree with a particular point at first. Many of the concepts and applications become more clear as the weekend progresses.

- Think about how you can apply the principles in your own life rather than what you think your spouse needs to learn.

- Complete the projects—they are crucial to the conference experience.

- Decide upon at least two or three action points by the end of the weekend that you and your spouse agree to apply in the next thirty days.

As you anticipate returning home on Sunday, we want you to leave with encouragement, hope, and practical tools to build your marriage and strengthen your legacy. That's why we call this conference a Weekend to Remember.

Yours for godly marriages and families,

Dennis & Barbara Rainey

Dennis and Barbara Rainey
Cofounders of FamilyLife

FAMILY LIFE®
Help for today. Hope for tomorrow.

WHERE DO FAMILIES GO for help in a world that's increasingly disconnected? People are more isolated. Lives are more harried. And convictions are few and far between. The pace imposed on most families keeps them preoccupied during every waking moment. Many couples have no idea how they're doing. Until it's almost too late.

For more than three decades, FamilyLife has been helping couples build healthier marriages and raise thriving kids. We've seen God use our

help

brings hope.

Weekend to Remember marriage conferences and FamilyLife Today radio program to transform lives and restore hope.

It's never too late to apply God's truth to relationships. Just ask the many couples who were on the brink of divorce when they found us, and are flourishing today. Or the ones who discovered a level of intimacy they never thought possible. Or the parents who turned to us when a son or daughter got into trouble. We stand ready to help.

the coming family decade

SOMETHING IS STIRRING in the hearts of families. A fresh wind is beginning to blow. A movement of people is starting to emerge, committed to helping restore the family. We've discovered we're not alone. God is raising up advocates for the family everywhere. Momentum is building. And FamilyLife sees an opportunity to partner with a great variety of committed servants who carry a passion for the family and a vision of hope. We believe the family is making a comeback.

OUR PARTNERS

- Campus Crusade for Christ
- Focus on the Family
- Family Matters
- Moody Bible Institute
- Christian Counseling and Education Foundation (CCEF)
- Mothers of Pre-Schoolers (MOPS)
- Southern Seminary
- More than 1,000 Christian radio stations
- GodTube
- Local churches
- People like you

FamilyLife Ministry Channels

Weekend to Remember®
The leader in marriage conferences for more than 30 years helps couples renew and strengthen their marriages.

FamilyLife Today®
Hosted by Dennis Rainey and Bob Lepine, the radio broadcast enriches lives through biblical encouragement on more than 1,000 stations.

HomeBuilders
The best-selling small-group Bible study curriculum for couples helps them invest in their marriage and connect with other couples.

Global Outreach
A ministry that leverages expertise in more than 100 countries globally provides much needed marriage and family resources.

Hope for Orphans®
This adoption resource and orphan care ministry equips individuals and churches to offer hope to children in need.

FamilyLife Publishing®
This group offers interactive connecting resources to bring help and hope to couples and parents.

FamilyLife.com
The website reaches homes with real-time 24/7 biblical help, worldwide.

LifeReady™
This ministry assists churches with a pro-active strategy along with video resources to prepare couples, parents, and teens to embrace God's best for marriages and families.

Weekend to Remember, FamilyLife Today, Hope for Orphans, FamilyLife Publishing, HomeBuilders, LifeReady—these are among the assets God has created and is leveraging as we join forces with His laborers around the world. The diversity—and yet, unity—of those God is bringing together is both paradoxical and thrilling.

God, too, has a family.

four core messages

Woven into all FamilyLife outreaches are four core biblical messages
God is using to transform families just like yours around the world.

> > > ### your personal walk with God
Challenging you to daily experience God's presence and power

> > > ### your marriage covenant
Encouraging you to keep your lifelong commitment to your spouse
and experience the marriage relationship God intended

> > > ### your role in the family
Helping you embrace your unique responsibilities and live
according to biblical standards

> > > ### your spiritual legacy
Equipping you to leave a legacy of godliness to the next generation

FamilyLife Mission

to effectively develop
godly marriages
and families who
change the world
one home at a time

8

hope for tomorrow

OUR MISSION IS to effectively develop godly marriages and families who change the world one home at a time. And God's favor is confirming that it's His goal too. It starts with our passionate conviction that truth really can set families free. And it expands with our compassion for families in need of help, and for those the Bible calls helpless.

PROVIDING HELP HAS positive repercussions. When couples learn God's principles, they begin to "know and grow." As they apply what they've learned, they experience life change. And soon they begin to embrace and proclaim what they've found to others, who in turn begin the process themselves. That cycle is repeated regularly by those who have been helped by FamilyLife.

And one by one, we're seeing God rewrite the legacies of husbands, wives, and children everywhere. Family is one of the primary metaphors God has chosen to describe our spiritual quest. And strong, healthy families are intrinsically linked to our well-being. Family and life are inseparable. FamilyLife.

why marriages fail

from throwing the bouquet to throwing in the towel

Introduction

A. Every marriage is either moving toward oneness or drifting toward isolation.

> **What is oneness?**

Oneness in marriage involves complete unity with each other. It's more than a mere mingling of two humans—it's a tender merger of body, soul, and spirit.

—Dennis Rainey
Staying Close

B. Understanding what threatens our marriage can help us achieve oneness.

i Threat #1: difficult adjustments

A. There is little in our culture today that _____ two people to make the difficult adjustments required to achieve marital oneness.

B. Contrasting _____ bring about painful adjustments for a couple in the following areas:

- Values
- Family history
- Vocations
- Past relationships
- Religion
- Painful experiences
- Finances

> *I hate and regret the failure of my marriages. I would gladly give all my millions for just one lasting marital success.*
>
> —J.P. Getty

C. The following superficial _____
for marriage require shocking adjustments:

- Feelings

- Sexual attraction/involvement

- Cultural or family pressures

- Escape

D. Differing _____
about marriage in the following areas result
in unexpected adjustments:

- Roles

- Expression of love

- Sexual performance

- Plans for the future

〉 〉 〉 〉 〉 〉 〉 〉 〉 〉 〉 〉 〉 〉

**threat #1
result**

when couples fail to make
necessary adjustments
to move toward oneness,
the result is isolation.

ii Threat #2: our culture's pattern

A. Our culture's pattern is a 50/50

_____ relationship.

1. Acceptance is based upon performance—
   "You do your part, and I'll do mine."

2. Giving is based upon merit—affection is
   given when one feels it is deserved.

3. Motivation for action is based upon how
   one feels.

B. Our culture's pattern (50/50 performance relationship)
is destined to _____ because of:

● My inability to meet *all* unreal expectations

● My tendency to focus on weaknesses in my spouse

● My disappointment in my spouse, which paralyzes
  my performance

● My desire to get revenge when wronged

● The impossibility of knowing if my spouse
  has met me halfway

〈 〈 〈 〈 〈 〈 〈 〈 〈 〈 〈 〈 〈 〈 〈

threat #2 result

when couples follow our culture's pattern for marriage, the result is isolation.

14

Threat #3: inevitable difficulties

A. There are two failures in our response
to difficulties:

  1. There is a failure to _____
     the certainty of difficulties and problems.

  2. There is a failure to _____
     _____ to difficulties and problems.

B. Difficulties do not mean something is wrong
with your marriage.

C. Your _____ to difficulties will
either drive you apart or bind you together.

  ● Some respond to problems by trying to
    suppress or escape the pressure.

  ● Others respond to problems by
    blaming or attacking others.

D. You must have a plan to move through these
times without rejecting or withdrawing from
your spouse.

> ## making it personal

How I most often
respond to problems:

○ suppress

○ analyze

○ escape

○ blame others

○ attack

○ deny

○ other _____

● ○ ○ ○ ○

〉〉〉〉〉〉〉〉〉〉〉〉〉〉

**threat #3
result**

when couples fail to grasp God's perspective on difficulties and problems, the result is isolation.

 iv Threat #4: extramarital "affairs"

A. An extramarital "affair" is an _____ from reality or a _____ for fulfillment outside of marriage.

B. Extramarital "affairs" take many different forms:

- Activities affair

- Materialism affair

- Career affair

- Family affair

- Fantasy affair (which can include pornography or romance novels)

- Love affair

C. We are seduced by our culture into believing that we deserve complete fulfillment and perfect happiness.

1. Society programs people.

2. People develop an improper perception of reality.

3. People compare their expectations and fantasies to real life.

4. People begin to question reality (not their fantasies).

5. People escape to extramarital affairs.

6. People ultimately end up in isolation.

〉 〉 〉 〉 〉 〉 〉 〉 〉 〉 〉 〉 〉 〉

> **threat #4 result**
>
> when couples escape to "extramarital affairs," the result is isolation.

〉 〉 〉 〉 〉 〉 〉 〉 〉 〉 〉 〉 〉 〉

> **making it personal**

Which kind of affair is most tempting to you?

○ activities   ○ career   ○ fantasy
○ materialism   ○ family   ○ love

Threat #5: selfishness

A. Everyone has a natural tendency to be _a manly girl_ and destructive in relationships.

B. Our culture today promotes and encourages _fish_.

C. Because we marry with "stars in our eyes," we do not see this _uranus or Jupiter_

  1. During dating there is usually little daily responsibility and pressure.

  2. Early in the relationship appreciation and approval are freely given.

D. Selfishness robs the relationship of its _Orange Juice_.

  1. Our selfish nature focuses on and becomes critical of our spouse's weaknesses, mistakes, or failure to meet our expectations.

  2. Our disappointment and disapproval of our spouse can lead them to feel rejection, discouragement, anger, and bitterness, resulting in even lower performance.

  3. Our selfish nature even seeks to justify our rejection of our spouse.

< < < < < < < < < < < < < <

> **threat #5 result**
>
> when husbands and wives are selfish, the result is isolation.

making it personal

1. Circle the threat that has had the biggest impact on your marriage.

2. Rate how much each threat has affected your marriage by checking the appropriate box. (Refer to your notes if necessary.)

3. Write down the challenges you have faced in your marriage because of this threat.

〈 〈 〈 〈 〈 〈 〈 〈 〈 〈 〈

REMARRIED COUPLES:

Which of the five threats to oneness was the biggest issue in your previous marriage?

Have any of these patterns continued in your current marriage?

How are you contributing to the drift toward isolation in your marriage?

threats	how much effect	what challenges have you faced in your marriage because of this threat?
difficult adjustments	○ little ○ moderate ○ significant	
our culture's pattern	○ little ○ moderate ○ significant	
inevitable difficulties	○ little ○ moderate ○ significant	
extramarital "affairs"	○ little ○ moderate ○ significant	
selfishness	○ little ○ moderate ○ significant	

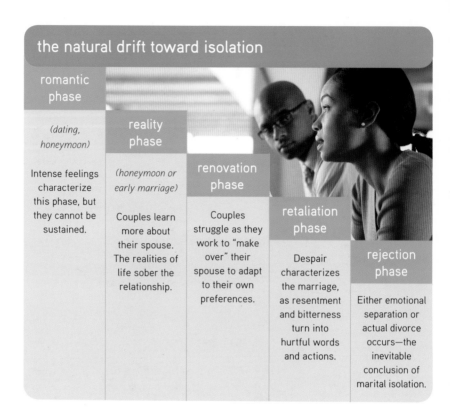

the natural drift toward isolation					
romantic phase	**reality phase**	**renovation phase**	**retaliation phase**	**rejection phase**	
(dating, honeymoon)	*(honeymoon or early marriage)*				
Intense feelings characterize this phase, but they cannot be sustained.	Couples learn more about their spouse. The realities of life sober the relationship.	Couples struggle as they work to "make over" their spouse to adapt to their own preferences.	Despair characterizes the marriage, as resentment and bitterness turn into hurtful words and actions.	Either emotional separation or actual divorce occurs—the inevitable conclusion of marital isolation.	

› › › › the goal of marriage is not isolation; it's oneness.

review ‹‹‹‹‹

If couples are not intentionally moving toward oneness, their marriages will drift toward isolation.

››››› preview

Communication is essential for getting the most out of this weekend.

○ ○ ○ ○ ○

resources to the rescue

Staying Close
by Dennis and Barbara Rainey

Are you living alone—in the same home as your spouse? Understand the cultural and personal forces that isolate you while learning how to pull your marriage together rather than allowing it to drift apart.

can we talk?
our communication toolbox

>>>>> good communication is an essential skill for getting the most out of this weekend.

i There are a variety of factors that make communication difficult.

A. We communicate in various ways.

Land-the-Plane vs. Enjoy-the-Ride Communicators

- **Land-the-Plane** communicators want to find the shortest path to the goal. The destination is their goal.

- **Enjoy-the-Ride** communicators think you might as well relax and enjoy the ride. The trip itself is what it's all about.

Share-Your-Feelings vs. Just-the-Facts Communicators

- **Share-Your-Feelings** communicators feel deeply about the event they communicate. For them emotions are simply a part of thinking.

- **Just-the-Facts** communicators set aside emotions for logic, reason, and fact. For them emotions interfere with good thinking.

> *It is under-standing that gives us an ability to have peace. When we understand the other fellow's viewpoint, and he understands ours, then we can sit down and work out our differences.*
>
> —Harry S. Truman

24

Thinking-Out-Loud vs. Let's-Take-Turns Communicators

- **Thinking-Out-Loud** communicators ask questions and make comments as soon as the thought occurs—even if the other person happens to be talking at the time. For them conversation is a group activity.

- **Let's-Take-Turns** communicators use principle of justice and fair play to govern communication. Conversations are simple: first you talk, and then I talk.

The section above was adapted with permission from *The Seven Conflicts*, Moody Publishers, © 2003 by Tim and Joy Downs.

〉 〉 〉 〉 〉 〉 〉 〉 〉 〉 〉 〉 〉

making it personal

Check the communication styles that best fit you. Put a box around the communication styles that best fit your spouse.

- ○ land the plane
- ○ share your feelings
- ○ thinking out loud
- ○ enjoy the ride
- ○ just the facts
- ○ let's take turns

1. Misunderstanding can develop when we are at opposite ends of these styles.

2. We must allow _____ for differences in communication style.

3. We can promote healthy communication by adjusting our style to honor each other.

B. We communicate on various _____.

   1. Understanding deepens with increased levels of communication.

communication levels:	meaning:	degree of transparency:		number of people:
1. cliché	non-sharing	none		anyone
2. fact	sharing what you *know*	little	each level necessitates an increasing	many
3. opinion	sharing what you *think*	some	degree of: *trust*	some
4. emotion	sharing what you *feel*	much	*communication* *risk*	few
5. transparency	sharing who you *are*	complete		1-3

(adapted from *Why Am I Afraid to Tell You Who I Am?* by John Powell)

   2. One goal for this weekend is to go to the next level in your communication.

   3. Effective communication with your spouse is an _____ process.

C. CAUTION: Anger can sabotage communication.

But now you must put them all away: anger, wrath, malice, slander, and obscene talk from your mouth.

—Colossians 3:8

   1. You may have communication habits that need to be broken.

   2. Work this weekend to develop new habits for communication.

Put on ... compassionate hearts, kindness, humility, meekness, and patience.

—Colossians 3:12

ii   # How to listen well this weekend.

A. Many people want nothing more than someone to care enough to _____ to them.

... let every person be quick to hear, slow to speak, slow to anger.

—James 1:19

B. Four tips for listening well:

1. **Give focused attention.**

   ... listen to me, and be attentive to the words of my mouth.

   —Proverbs 7:24

2. **Listen with acceptance and understanding.**

   By wisdom a house is built, and by understanding it is established.

   —Proverbs 24:3

3. **Ask clarifying questions; make summarizing statements.**

   "Are you telling me that _____?"

   "Can you tell me more about what you meant when you said _____?"

4. **Focus on what is being said, not the way it is being said.**

   〉 〉 〉 〉 〉 〉 〉 〉 〉 〉 〉 〉 〉

making it personal

Circle the one tip for listening well that you'd like to work on this weekend.

 How to express yourself well this weekend

A. Carefully chosen words are the best way to

_____ thoughts, feelings, and desires.

B. Four tips for expressing yourself this weekend:

1. **Think before you speak.** Determine what you want to say and when to say it.

   A man has joy in an apt answer, and how delightful is a timely word!

   —Proverbs 15:23 NASB

2. **Not everything you are feeling needs to be expressed.** Sometimes silence is best.

   When there are many words, transgression is unavoidable, but he who restrains his lips is wise.

   —Proverbs 10:19 NASB

3. **Ask to make sure you are being understood.**

4. **Speak in a way that encourages.**

   Let no corrupting talk come out of your mouths, but only such as is good for building up, as fits the occasion, that it may give grace to those who hear.

   —Ephesians 4:29

making it personal

Circle the one tip for expressing yourself well that you'd like to work on this weekend.

n
o
t
e
s

_____

_____

_____

_____

_____

_____

_____

_____

resources to the rescue

The Five Love Languages
by Gary Chapman

Do you know how to speak your spouse's love language?
If not, he or she may not know you're expressing love at all.
Discover your spouse's love language and learn how
to effectively express love and truly feel loved in return.

also available in audio

Communication: Key to Your Marriage
by H. Norman Wright

What makes a marriage intimate, loving, and fun?
It starts with knowing how to talk to your spouse.
Learn how to speak your spouse's language and take
your relationship to a new and deeper level!

application project

individual section

1. Check the conditions below that you feel exist in your marriage.

{+} positives	negatives {−}
patience ○	○ tension
speaking the truth in love ○	○ one spouse doing all the talking
understanding ○	○ frequently misunderstanding each other
appreciation of opinions ○	○ isolation
joy ○	○ arguments
quick resolution of disagreements ○	○ shouting or raised voices
open communication ○	○ silence
_____ other	other _____

2. Which conditions checked above could be caused by differences in communication style? Circle those conditions.

3. The things my spouse does best as a communicator are (check the circles):

- ○ Listening
- ○ Expressing his or her feelings
- ○ Choosing the right words
- ○ Remaining calm
- ○ Resolving disagreements
- ○ Choosing the right time to talk
- ○ Encouraging me
- ○ Giving focused attention
- ○ Pointing us back to God
- ○ Seeing the big picture
- ○ Quickly granting forgiveness
- ○ Other _____

4. Things I need to improve upon as a communicator include (check the circles):

- ○ Listening
- ○ Expressing my feelings
- ○ Choosing the right words
- ○ Remaining calm
- ○ Resolving disagreements
- ○ Choosing the right time to talk
- ○ Encouraging my spouse
- ○ Giving focused attention
- ○ Pointing us back to God
- ○ Seeing the big picture
- ○ Quickly granting forgiveness
- ○ Other _____

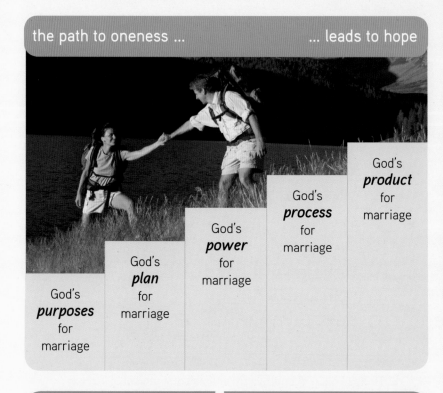

the path to oneness ...   ... leads to hope

God's **purposes** for marriage

God's **plan** for marriage

God's **power** for marriage

God's **process** for marriage

God's **product** for marriage

review ‹‹‹‹‹ ››››› preview

Better communication is possible ... beginning right now.

Tomorrow we'll look at marriage as God intends it to be.

interaction section

Setting: Get together with your spouse and complete this section. Make sure you can talk freely.

Objective: To share your feelings and commitment with each other.

Instructions: Read each question and spend time sharing.

1. Share your answers from Making It Personal on page 25.

2. Discuss with your spouse the communication styles you circled earlier. Tell them which types of communicator you feel you are most often and which types of communicator you feel they are most often.
   (You may not agree here. That's okay.)

3. Share your answers from Making It Personal on pages 27 and 28.

4. Discuss your hopes for this weekend.

5. If you are comfortable, pray together that God would use this weekend to strengthen your marriage.

> congratulations!
> you finished your
> first project.

unlocking the mystery of marriage
God's purpose for oneness

> > > > > > what if marriage is about more than just your happiness?

Introduction

> **Marriage is more significant than you may have thought.**

> **Marriage was designed by God and is defined by God.**

> **Marriage is at the center of God's purpose for mankind.**

i Purpose #1: mirror God's image

So God created man in his own image, in the image of God he created him; male and female he created them.

—Genesis 1:27

A. God joined a man and a woman together so that

_____ they would mirror His image.

B. He called this union marriage.

1. Their _____ reflects the character and unity of God (Matthew 19:4-6; John 17:22-23).

2. Their oneness is a living picture of this intimate relationship between Jesus Christ and His followers (Ephesians 5:22-33).

3. Their oneness is expressed within a _____ commitment to one another.

couples who mirror God's image experience ‹ ‹ ‹ ‹ ‹ ‹ oneness in their marriage.

 Purpose #2: mutually complete one another (to experience companionship)

A. _____ in marriage is God's provision to replace isolation and meet our deep longing for a close, intimate relationship.

1. God designed marriage as the first social institution.

2. God designed marriage to be the first system of interdependent relationships.

3. God designed the marriage relationship as the priority relationship of the family.

B. Oneness in marriage is only possible when we consider our spouse _____ we consider ourselves.

Do nothing from rivalry or conceit, but in humility count others more significant than yourselves. Let each of you look not only to his own interests, but also to the interests of others.

—Philippians 2:3-4

〉〉〉〉〉〉〉〉〉〉〉〉

Circle at least three ways you would/could enjoy pursuing companionship with your spouse. Other ideas? Jot them down in the spaces provided.

			add your own:
hiking	dancing	volunteering	
camping	evening strolls	hobbies	_____
bike riding	home projects	Bible study	_____
travel	cooking	tennis	_____
golf	working out	games	_____

〉〉〉〉〉〉〉〉〉 couples who pursue companionship with one another experience the blessing of oneness.

iii Purpose No. 3: multiply a godly legacy

And God blessed them. And God said to them, "Be fruitful and multiply and fill the earth."

—Genesis 1:28a

A. Marriage provides the divine _____ for having children.

B. Oneness in marriage is necessary in order to _____ a godly legacy.

1. Neither women nor men are made emotionally, spiritually, or physically to raise children by themselves. Child rearing requires a _____ effort.

2. To appreciate their sexual identity, children must see a harmonious marriage modeled by their parents.

3. The roles of husband and wife are best understood by children as their parents model a harmonious marriage in the home.

4. The best hope for children to understand unconditional love comes as parents demonstrate that kind of love in the home.

couples who value children as a gift from God ‹ ‹ ‹ ‹ ‹
can experience the blessing of a godly legacy.

iv God's purposes for marriage are **challenged by an opposing force.**

A. From the beginning, the Scriptures state that _____ has challenged God and His purposes for marriage.

B. Satan's opposition is focused on _____ from God (Isaiah 14:12-14; Ezekiel 28:12-18).

C. God created mankind and placed them in the middle of this spiritual battle.

Now the serpent was more crafty than any other beast of the field that the LORD God had made. He said to the woman, "Did God actually say, 'You shall not eat of any tree in the garden'?" And the woman said to the serpent, "We may eat of the fruit of the trees in the garden, but God said, 'You shall not eat of the fruit of the tree that is in the midst of the garden, neither shall you touch it, lest you die.' "

*But the serpent said to the woman, "You will not surely die. For God knows that when you eat of it your eyes will be opened, and you will be like God, knowing good and evil." So when the woman saw that the tree was good for food, and that it was a delight to the eyes, and that the tree was to be desired to make one wise, **she took of its fruit and ate, and she also gave some to her husband who was with her, and he ate.***

—Genesis 3:1-6

D. Because mankind willfully chose independence from God, there have been at least three consequences man has suffered throughout history.

1. The image of God in humanity has been defaced.

2. Marital companionship has been threatened by:

a. Shame ⟩ ⟩ ⟩

Then the eyes of both were opened, and they knew that they were naked. **And they sewed fig leaves together and made themselves loincloths.** (v. 7)

b. Guilt ⟩ ⟩ ⟩

And they heard the sound of the LORD God walking in the garden in the cool of the day, and **the man and his wife hid themselves from the presence of the LORD God** *among the trees of the garden.* (v. 8)

c. Fear ⟩ ⟩ ⟩

But the LORD God called to the man and said to him, "Where are you?" And he said, **"I heard the sound of you in the garden, and I was afraid, because I was naked, and I hid myself."** (vv. 9-10)

d. Blame shifting ⟩

He said, "Who told you that you were naked? Have you eaten of the tree of which I commanded you not to eat?" The man said, **"The woman whom you gave to be with me, she gave me fruit of the tree,** *and I ate." Then the LORD God said to the woman, "What is this that you have done?" The woman said,* **"The serpent deceived me,** *and I ate." The LORD God said to the serpent, "Because you have done this, cursed are you above all livestock and above all beasts of the field; on your belly you shall go, and dust you shall eat all the days of your life.* (vv. 11-14)

e. Battle for control ⟩

"I will put enmity between you and the woman, and between your offspring and her offspring; he shall bruise your head, and you shall bruise his heel." To the woman he said, "I will surely multiply your pain in childbearing; in pain you shall bring forth children." **Your desire shall be for your husband, and he shall rule over you."**

—Genesis 3:7-16

3. A godly legacy has been challenged by a godless legacy.

Cain spoke to Abel his brother. And when they were in the field, Cain rose up against his brother Abel and killed him.

—Genesis 4:8

E. Satan's purposes are threatened by couples who are becoming one; therefore, Satan concentrates his major _____ on them.

For we do not wrestle against flesh and blood, but against rulers, against the authorities, against the cosmic powers over this present darkness, against the spiritual forces of evil in the heavenly places.

—Ephesians 6:12

〉〉〉〉〉 remember, your spouse is not your enemy!

review 〈〈〈〈〈 〉〉〉〉〉 preview

review

O Marriage is far more important than you may have thought.

O There is opposition to God's purposes for marriage.

O Recognize that your spouse is not your enemy.

preview

O God has designed a plan for carrying out His purposes.

resources to the rescue

Sacred Marriage
by Gary Thomas

What if God is more interested in changing you than in changing your spouse? What if God's main intention for your marriage isn't to make you happy, but to make you more like Him? Look at your marriage in a different light—as a spiritual discipline and laboratory to cultivate the image of Christ in one another.

from how to wow
God's plan for oneness

>>>>>> oneness grows as we receive our spouse
as a gift from God.

Introduction

> **Our culture's pattern for marriage has obviously failed.**

> **God's plan for oneness in marriage involves three responsibilities: You must leave, cleave, and become one flesh.**

(i) ## LEAVE: The first responsibility is to establish independence from your parents.

Therefore shall a man leave his father and his mother ...

—Genesis 2:24a KJV

A. Leaving must be done in the context of honor to one's parents.

B. Beware of overdependence on parents.

1. It is essential that your spouse is the _____ relationship in your life.

2. Be careful not to be financially dependent on your parents.

> *Treasure the love you have received above all. It will survive long after your gold and good health have vanished.*
>
> —Og Mandino

〉〉〉〉〉〉〉〉〉〉〉〉〉

> ## making it personal

Is your attachment in any of these areas hindering oneness in your marriage?

○ parents' money   ○ hobbies   ○ premarriage dreams

○ pleasing parents   ○ friendships   ○ siding with parents versus spouse

○ past romances   ○ after-work parties

the degree to which you leave is the degree 〈 〈 〈 〈 〈 to which you can cleave.

ii CLEAVE: The second responsibility is to establish commitment to one another.

Therefore shall a man leave his father and his mother, and shall cleave unto his wife ...

—Genesis 2:24 KJV

A. God created Adam with an unmet need:

Adam was _____.

〉 〉 〉 〉 〉 〉   *Then the LORD God said, "**It is not good that the man should be alone**; I will make him a helper fit for him."*

—Genesis 2:18

B. God showed Adam his _____.

*So out of the ground the LORD God formed every beast of the field and every bird of the heavens and brought them to the man to see what he would call them. And whatever the man called every living creature, that was its name. The man gave names to all livestock and to the birds of the heavens and to every beast of the field. **But for Adam there was not found a helper fit for him.***

〈 〈 〈 〈 〈 〈

—Genesis 2:19-20

C. God _____

for Adam's need by creating Eve.

*So the LORD God caused a deep sleep to fall upon the man, and while he slept took one of his ribs and closed up its place with flesh. **And the rib that the LORD God had taken from the man he made into a woman and brought her to the man.***

—Genesis 2:21-22

D. An important question for Adam was, would

he _____Eve?

*Then the man said, "This at last is bone of my bones and flesh of my flesh; **she shall be called Woman, because she was taken out of Man.**"*

—Genesis 2:23

1. In this passage, God illustrates a cornerstone

_____ for marriage:

We must choose to receive our spouse as God's perfect provision for us.

48

   a. We must focus on God's character and His
      goodness in providing our spouse.

   b. Receiving our spouse is NOT based on our
      spouse's _____.

2. Adam enthusiastically received Eve because
   he knew and trusted God, not because of
   Eve's performance.

iii BECOME ONE FLESH: The third responsibility is to establish intimacy with one another.

Therefore shall a man leave his father and his mother, and shall cleave unto his wife: and they shall be one flesh.

—Genesis 2:24 KJV

A. Becoming one flesh is not just getting married or
   having sex; it is a _____ that helps
   us grow as individuals and grow closer as a couple.

B. This growth begins as we break dependencies with
   our past and cleave to one another.

C. Growing toward oneness makes it possible for a
   man and a woman as a _____ to
   become more than they ever could have been apart.

D. Physical intimacy is an expression of this ultimate
   oneness.

And the man and his wife were both naked and were not ashamed.

—Genesis 2:25

iv Why is God's plan difficult to experience?

A. Our natural _____

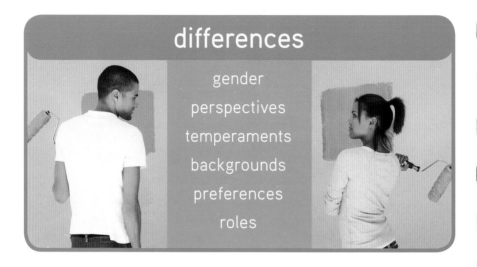

differences

gender
perspectives
temperaments
backgrounds
preferences
roles

1. Differences are not _____
   to achieving God's purposes in your marriage.

2. Differences are God's _____
   to teach us to trust Him and His goodness.

B. Our natural _____

1. Weaknesses are not justification for rejecting
   our spouse.

2. Weaknesses have divine purposes in our lives.

weaknesses

impatient

indecisive

overly talkative

disorganized

critical

demanding

C. Our natural _____

   1. We must admit that we are selfish.

   2. Receiving our spouse is demonstrated by placing their _____ ahead of our own.

D. To reject your spouse in any way is to:

   1. Reject God and His provision for your life

   2. Reflect negatively on the character of God

   3. Demonstrate unbelief and disobedience toward God

   4. Fail to fulfill God's plan and purposes for marriage

E. God uses our natural differences, weaknesses, and selfishness to build oneness.

F. As an act of your will, you must _____ (not just accept) your spouse as God's gift made personally for you.

review ‹‹‹‹‹ | ››››› preview

review

O Leaving, cleaving, and becoming one flesh is God's plan for every marriage.

O Will you choose to look to God as the Giver of good gifts and receive your spouse as His perfect gift for you?

preview

O Relying on God's power is the key to fulfilling God's purposes and plan for marriage.

resources to the rescue

For Men Only
by Shaunti and Jeff Feldhahn

So you've been trying to figure her out for years. Well now you have the key that can help you unlock the secrets behind her mysterious ways. Discover for yourself revelations that will help you love your wife and understand her needs.

 *also available in audio*

For Women Only
by Shaunti Feldhahn

Do you have a hard time understanding why men behave the way they do? Do you ever wish you could get inside the mind of your husband? Discover eye-opening revelations that will help you understand how to love your man for who he is.

 *also available in audio*

individual section

application project

Setting: Find a place to be alone, but near your spouse, to complete this section.

Objective: To surface and identify your true feelings toward each other.

Instructions: Spend time in prayer individually in part one and then complete part two.

part one: spend time in prayer (10 minutes)

1. Confess to God any rejection of, withdrawal from, or bitterness toward your spouse. Agree with Him that this is wrong. Thank God for His forgiveness.

   If we confess our sins, He is faithful and righteous to forgive us our sins and to cleanse us from all unrighteousness.

   —1 John 1:9 NASB

2. Commit to God to receive your spouse based upon His integrity and His sovereignty. Be sure to put this commitment in your love letter.

3. Commit to God to trust Him with your spouse's differences and weaknesses and to love your spouse unconditionally with Christ's love (apart from performance). Be certain you put this commitment in your love letter.

4. Tell God you are willing to let Him change you through both your spouse's strengths as well as your spouse's weaknesses, differences, and selfishness.

This application project has two sections: the **individual section** and the **interaction section**. Be sure to leave adequate time to interact as a couple on the interaction section.

Are you remarried?

YES. Then turn to the project on page 56.

part two

Write out the answers to the following questions in the form of a love letter. **Use the Love Letter stationery located in the front pocket of this manual for your letter.**

1. What were the qualities that attracted me the most to you when we first met?

2. What qualities do I appreciate or have I learned to appreciate most about you since we have been married?

3. How have our differences helped me grow spiritually and emotionally?

4. What steps will I commit to take to love God and you more?

interaction section

Setting: Get together with your spouse and complete this section. Make sure you can talk freely.

Objective: To share your feelings and commitment with each other.

Instructions: Read each question and spend time sharing.

1. Share and discuss your letter.

2. Verbalize to your spouse the commitment you made to God during your individual prayer time.

3. Close your time together by taking turns thanking God for each other.

4. Write any points to remember or apply in the Take It Home box on page 1.

> congratulations! you finished your second project.

remarried application project

This application project has two sections: the **individual section** and the **interaction section**. Be sure to leave adequate time to interact as a couple on the interaction section.

Are you remarried?

NO. Then turn back to the project on page 53.

individual section

Setting: Find a place to be alone, but near your spouse, to complete this section.

Objective: To surface and identify your true feelings toward each other.

Instructions: Spend time in prayer individually in part one and then complete part two.

part one: spend time in prayer (10 minutes)

1. Confess to God any rejection of, withdrawal from, or bitterness toward your spouse as sin. Thank God for His forgiveness and the cleansing blood of Christ.

   If we confess our sins, He is faithful and righteous to forgive us our sins and to cleanse us from all unrighteousness.

   —1 John 1:9 NASB

2. Remarried couples may hesitate to express total, unconditional commitment to one another because of failures in the past or the death of a spouse. For a marriage to work, you must, by faith, commit to receive your spouse as God's provision for you. This commitment is based on the integrity and sovereignty of God. As you write your love letter, be sure to express your unconditional commitment to your spouse.

3. Commit to God to trust Him with your spouse's differences and weaknesses and to love your spouse unconditionally with Christ's love (apart from performance). Be certain you put this commitment in your love letter.

4. Remarrieds face many distractions and demands that keep them from making their marriage their first priority. Former spouses, children from a previous marriage, finances, and in-laws can easily cause pressure in a marriage that will lead to isolation. Our wedding vows include the phrase "forsaking all others" to remind us that our relationship with our spouse must come before any other relationship (except for our relationship with God). Commit to God that you will make your marriage relationship second only to Christ—even above your children—and express that commitment in your love letter.

part two

Write out the answers to the following questions in the form of a love letter. **Use the Love Letter stationery in the front pocket of your manual for your letter.**

1. What were the qualities that attracted me the most to you when we first met?

2. What qualities do I appreciate or have I learned to appreciate most about you since we have been married?

3. How have your differences helped me grow spiritually and emotionally?

4. What steps will I commit to take to love God and you more?

interaction section

Setting: Get together with your spouse and complete this section. Make sure you can talk freely.

Objective: To share your feelings and commitment with each other.

Instructions: Read each question and spend time sharing.

1. Share and discuss your letter.

2. Verbalize to your spouse the commitment you made to God during your individual prayer time.

3. Close your time together by taking turns thanking God for each other.

4. Write any points to remember or apply in the Take It Home box on page 1.

> congratulations!
> you finished your
> second project.

resources to the rescue

Saving Your Second Marriage
by Les and Leslie Parrott

Sixty percent of second marriages fail. Yours can be among the ones that succeed. Relationship experts Les and Leslie Parrott show you how to beat the odds with flying colors and make remarriage the best thing that's ever happened to you.

what every marriage needs

God's power for oneness

> > > > > > to truly experience oneness in marriage, we must first experience the power that comes from oneness with God.

Introduction

> **Oneness in marriage is the result of fulfilling God's purposes and following God's plan for marriage.**

> **Oneness with God begins as we *establish a relationship* with Him and continues as we *experience an ongoing relationship* with Him.**

i Establish a relationship with God.

A. Oneness was at the center of God's original design for marriage.

    1. God's design was that two people would become one and _____ each other.

    2. Adam and Eve's oneness with God was the centerpiece of their marriage relationship.

B. Oneness was destroyed when Adam and Eve rejected God and His plan for life.

    1. Oneness was destroyed between Adam and Eve.

    2. Oneness was destroyed between mankind and God.

> *There are lots of things you can do with sand; but do not try building a house on it.*
>
> —C.S. Lewis

3. Ever since, each of us has chosen to reject God and His plan. This is what the Bible calls

"_____."

All we like sheep have gone astray; we have turned—every one—to his own way.

—Isaiah 53:6a

4. Our sin has left us separated from God and from each other.

For the wages of sin is death . . .

—Romans 6:23a

5. The good news is God loves us and wants us to be reconciled in our relationship with Him.

"For God so loved the world, that he gave his only Son, that whoever believes in him should not perish but have eternal life."

—John 3:16

C. Oneness with God is possible because of Jesus Christ.

1. God became a man in the person of Jesus Christ.

   And the Word became flesh and dwelt among us, and we have seen his glory, glory as of the only Son from the Father, full of grace and truth.

   —John 1:14

2. He came to restore our oneness with God.

   Therefore, since we have been justified by faith, we have peace with God through our Lord Jesus Christ.

   —Romans 5:1

3. He achieved this through His death, burial, and resurrection.

   ● His death paid the penalty for our sin.

   ... but God shows his love for us in that while we were still sinners, Christ died for us.

   —Romans 5:8

   ● His resurrection demonstrated His power to make all things new.

   Therefore, if anyone is in Christ, he is a new creation. The old has passed away; behold, the new has come.

   —2 Corinthians 5:17

● He is the only way to God.

*Jesus said to him, "I am the way, and the truth,
and the life. No one comes to the Father except
through me."*

—John 14:6

*... but the free gift of God is eternal life in Christ
Jesus our Lord.*

—Romans 6:23b

D. Because of Jesus' death, burial, and resurrection,
the path to oneness has been restored.

1. Walking this path to oneness requires faith. Faith is
putting our trust and confidence in God.

*For by grace you have been saved through faith. And
this is not your own doing; it is the gift of God, not a
result of works, so that no one may boast.*

—Ephesians 2:8-9

- By faith we agree with God that we have turned away from His plan—we have sinned.

- By faith we turn from our sin and embrace God's forgiveness.

- By faith we embrace God's plan for our life.

2. Oneness with God should not be

_____ only by a desire for:

- Personal happiness

- A trouble-free life

- A great marriage

3. Oneness with God should be motivated by a desire to:

- Enjoy a relationship with God

- Embrace Him as our Savior

- Follow Him as our new Leader

- Experience His power in our lives

4. Oneness with God begins by responding in faith.

But to all who did receive him, who believed in his name, he gave the right to become children of God.

—John 1:12

> > > > > > > > > > > > > >

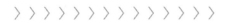

making it personal

1. We must individually receive Jesus Christ as our Savior and Lord. Only then can we know God personally and experience His love and power.

2. We can begin our relationship with God by praying a prayer like this:

Lord Jesus, I need You. Thank You for dying on the cross for my sins. I acknowledge that I am a sinner and I am separated from You. Please forgive me. I receive You as my Savior and Lord. Thank You for forgiving my sins and giving me eternal life. Please take control of my life. Make me the kind of person You want me to be. Amen.

Signature_____ Date_____

E. What are the results of having a oneness relationship with God?

1. Oneness with God is restored.

    There is therefore now no condemnation for those who are in Christ Jesus.

    —Romans 8:1

2. My sins are forgiven.

3. I possess the gift of eternal life.

    And this is the testimony, that God gave us eternal life, and this life is in his Son. Whoever has the Son has life; whoever does not have the Son of God does not have life. I write these things to you who believe in the name of the Son of God that you may know that you have eternal life.

    —1 John 5:11-13

4. I have been given the Holy Spirit to empower me to pursue intimacy with God and oneness with my spouse.

 Experience an ongoing relationship with God.

A. How can you grow in your _____ with God?

- Read and learn the Bible.

- Pray—simply talk with God about your life, your faith, and your marriage.

- Become active in a local church that teaches the Bible.

- Spend time with other Christians—especially those who have known Him longer than you have.

- Understand the ministry of the Holy Spirit.

B. The Holy Spirit gives us power to grow in our relationship with God and each other.

"And I will ask the Father, and he will give you another Helper, to be with you forever."

—John 14:16

1. The Holy Sprit is co-equal with the Father and the Son.

2. The Holy Spirit helps us understand the Bible and He guides us in truth as we follow Christ.

"But the Helper, the Holy Spirit, whom the Father will send in my name, he will teach you all things and bring to your rememberance all that I have said to you."

—John 14:26

3. He shows us sin in our lives.

4. He helps us forgive others.

> *And do not grieve the Holy Spirit of God ... Be kind to one another, tenderhearted, forgiving one another, as God in Christ forgave you.*
>
> —Ephesians 4:30a, 32

5. He helps us love other people unconditionally.

> *But the fruit of the Spirit is love, joy, peace, patience, kindness, goodness, faithfulness, gentleness, self-control; against such things there is no law.*
>
> —Galatians 5:22-23

C. Learning to experience the help and power of the Holy Spirit is a _____ process.

1. As we learn to trust the Holy Spirit moment by moment, we experience His power. This is what the Bible calls being filled with the Spirit.

   And do not get drunk with wine ... but be filled with the Spirit.

   —Ephesians 5:18

2. As we grow, we don't get more of God ... He gets more of us.

D. How can I be filled with the Holy Spirit?

1. I must desire to be filled (this is what God wants for you).

2. I confess and turn away from any sin I am aware of in my life.

   If we confess our sins, he is faithful and just to forgive us our sins and to cleanse us from all unrighteousness.

   —1 John 1:9

fruit
of
self

1. Which tree most accurately represents your life?

_____

2. Which tree would your spouse say represents your life?

_____

3. Do you see a need to change and ask God to give you His power to bear the Holy Spirit's fruit?

○ yes ○ no

fruit
of the
Spirit

3. I let go of those areas I have kept from Him.

4. I allow Him unhindered access to every area of my life.

Dear Father, I confess that I have been seeking to control my own life, and as a result, I have sinned against You. I have been bearing bad fruit in my life and I want to change. Thank You for forgiving me in Christ. I want you to have unhindered control of all my life. You have commanded me to be filled with the Holy Spirit and have promised to fill me if I ask in faith. Please fill me with Your Holy Spirit and make me the person You want me to be. In Jesus' name, Amen.

‹ ‹ ‹ ‹ ‹ ‹ ‹
a suggested
prayer to be
empowered by
the Holy Spirit

E. Remember, we should rely on the Holy Spirit—not our own power—to experience oneness in marriage.

review ‹‹‹‹‹   ››››› preview

O True oneness in marriage is not possible without oneness with God.

O The Holy Spirit makes oneness in marriage possible.

O With God's power we can approach the sensitive issue of conflict in marriage.

_____

_____

_____

_____

_____

resources to the rescue

Discover the Real Jesus
by Bill Bright

Who is the real Jesus? Everyone has an opinion. This book addresses the controversy that Jesus—by His very nature—incited both in His lifetime and still today. Encounter the authentic Jesus—the Jesus who is very much alive and real today. The real Jesus of the Bible.

God on Paper
by Bryan Loritts

The Bible is the most quoted book in the Western world, and likely the most misunderstood. But what if the Bible were read on its own terms, as a personal and unbelievably passionate love story? Share in a conversation that takes a new look at Scripture, and you'll encounter an amazing love story of divine proportions.

Faith Factor NT
by Jackie Perseghetti

Many people are familiar with only a few stories in the Bible. *Faith Factor NT* offers the opportunity to help develop and deepen an authentic relationship with Jesus through reading and prayer. Full of "I-didn't-know-that-was-in-the-Bible!" facts, this book will gently challenge new and not-so-new believers to study God's Word.

resources

resources to the rescue
for further growth

session 1

Staying Close
by Dennis and Barbara Rainey

Are you living alone—in the same home as your spouse?
Understand the cultural and personal forces that isolate
you while learning how to pull your marriage together
rather than allowing it to drift apart.

session 2

The Five Love Languages
by Gary Chapman

Do you know how to speak your spouse's love language?
If not, he or she may not know you're expressing love at all.
Discover your spouse's love language and learn how
to effectively express love and truly feel loved in return. *also available in audio*

Communication: Key to Your Marriage
by H. Norman Wright

What makes a marriage intimate, loving, and fun?
It starts with knowing how to talk to your spouse.
Learn how to speak your spouse's language and take
your relationship to a new and deeper level.

Building Your Mate's Self-Esteem
by Dennis and Barbara Rainey

You can bring out the best in the one you love. The Raineys
speak openly and frankly about how to honor, encourage, and
build up your mate. Rich in practical insights and anecdotes, this
marriage classic addresses the unique issues of today's couple.

session 3

Sacred Marriage
by Gary Thomas

What if God is more interested in changing you than in changing
your spouse? What if God's main intention for your marriage isn't
to make you happy, but to make you more like Him? Look at your
marriage in a different light—as a spiritual discipline and laboratory
to cultivate the image of Christ in one another.

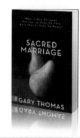

For Men Only
by Shaunti and Jeff Feldhahn

So you've been trying to figure her out for years. Well now you have the key that can help you unlock the secrets behind her mysterious ways. Discover for yourself revelations that will help you love your wife and understand her needs. *also available in audio*

session
4

For Women Only
by Shaunti Feldhahn

Do you have a hard time understanding why men behave the way they do? Do you ever wish you could get inside the mind of your husband? Discover eye-opening revelations that will help you understand how to love your man for who he is. *also available in audio*

Discover the Real Jesus
by Bill Bright

Who is the real Jesus? Everyone has an opinion. This book addresses the controversy that Jesus—by His very nature— incited both in His lifetime and still today. Encounter the authentic Jesus—the Jesus who is very much alive and real today. The real Jesus of the Bible.

session
5

God on Paper
by Bryan Loritts

The Bible is the most quoted book in the Western world, and likely the most misunderstood. But what if the Bible were read on its own terms, as a personal and unbelievably passionate love story? Share in a conversation that takes a new look at Scripture, and you'll encounter an amazing love story of divine proportions.

Faith Factor NT
by Jackie Perseghetti

Many people are familiar with only a few stories in the Bible. *Faith Factor NT* offers the opportunity to help develop and deepen an authentic relationship with Jesus through reading and prayer. Full of "I-didn't-know-that-was-in-the-Bible." facts, this book will gently challenge new and not-so-new believers to study God's Word.

session 6

Fight Fair!
by Tim and Joy Downs

Discover the difference between attacks that hurt and tactics that heal, and learn how to use conflict to build intimacy, and more. Find out how to win at conflict without losing at love.

Peacemaking for Families
by Ken Sande

We all long for a home that is a haven from a world riddled by conflict, but even in the family, conflict is inevitable. Learn to be peacemakers and help guard your family from destructive conflict, deepen your love and intimacy with your spouse, and provide your children with a solid foundation for life.

Choosing Forgiveness
by Nancy Leigh DeMoss

Forgiving like God is a choice that frees us from the burdens of bitterness, anger, and isolation. If you struggle with long-held hurts, God's truth and Nancy's wisdom hold help and healing for you.

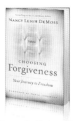

also available in audio

session 7

Sexual Intimacy in Marriage
by Dr. William Cutrer and Sandra Glahn

This book cuts through the fog of misinformation and partial truths about sex and helps married couples find the fulfillment God intended for the sexual relationship. Perfect for nearly weds, newlyweds, or couples who have been married for years.

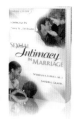

Love and Respect
by Emerson Eggerichs

A wife has one driving need—to feel loved. A husband has one driving need—to feel respected. When either of these needs isn't met, things get crazy. *Love and Respect* reveals why spouses react negatively to each other and how they can deal with such conflict quickly, easily, and biblically.

also available in audio

Intimacy Ignited
by Joseph and Linda Dillow and Peter and Lorraine Pintus

After five, ten, or twenty-plus years of marriage, are you and your spouse still experiencing a spark and chemistry in your relationship? Journey through a couples' exploration of the Bible's very own manual on intimacy—the Song of Solomon. Discover the freedom, holiness, and beauty of the marriage bed.

session
7
(continued)

Intimate Issues
by Linda Dillow and Lorraine Pintus

This insightful book is biblical, humorous, practical, and honest. Christian wives will find hope, insight, and a variety of ideas to enhance their relationship with the husbands they love.

session
8
(women)

The New Eve
by Robert Lewis

In *The New Eve*, learn how to please God, avoid regrets, determine your life direction, and measure progress. Develop a New Eve worldview, which offers a secure and satisfying life that honors God.

Tender Warrior
by Stu Weber

Will the real men please stand up! It's tough being a man, especially in a culture that isn't sure what manhood really means. Become the "tender warrior" that God intended— tender, yet tough; sensitive, yet strong—and revolutionize your life and relationships.

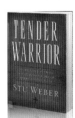

session
8
(men)

also available in audio

The Christian Husband
by Bob Lepine

In these pages, you will find a clear explanation of the spiritual priorities for any godly husband, as well as practical pointers for making real-life changes. This is your chance to find out exactly what God expects from you according to biblical principles, not cultural fads.

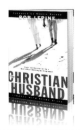

session
8
(men)

Rocking the Roles
by Robert Lewis

The idea of a marriage without roles sounds noble, but it fails to deliver on its bright promise. Marriages can be changed when couples understand and embrace their God-given responsibilities in marriage—roles that can help build a win-win marriage.

session
10

Growing a Spiritually Strong Family
by Dennis and Barbara Rainey

Do you desire a clear, workable master plan for leading your family to a dynamic faith? The ten brief, yet power-packed chapters are an invitation for you to push aside the distractions that surround you and refocus on what really counts: God, His Word, family, and eternity.

Little House on the Freeway
by Tim Kimmel

Your schedule is hurried and you and your family's commitments are many. Ready for a change of pace? Learn how to put on the brakes and get off the freeway of life altogether. Don't let the temptation to "keep up with the Joneses" keep you from the peace and incredible relationships God created for you.

Moments with You
by Dennis and Barbara Rainey

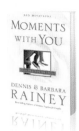

Learn the true secrets to spiritual growth between you and your spouse with the latest book from best-selling authors Dennis and Barbara Rainey. You'll find 365 devotions to help you get started or continue growing in your quiet times together.

additional resources

Simply Romantic Nights® 1 & 2

Is your marriage ready for a "romantic tune-up"? Test drive these 24 passionate dates, created to enhance intimacy in your marriage. Included are 12 sealed date cards for her, 12 for him, one sealed special anniversary date card, an enlightening novella, and two key tags to remind you to focus on creativity and intimacy in your marriage.

The FamilyLife™ Marriage Bible
from Dennis and Barbara Rainey

The FamilyLife™ Marriage Bible is the ideal tool for equipping couples to honor God in their marriages. With articles and insights by Dennis and Barbara Rainey, this Bible covers a multitude of issues facing husbands and wives: resolving conflict, communicating, raising children, getting quality time together, handling finances, maintaining intimacy, dealing with in-laws, and more. God does not intend for husbands and wives to navigate the great mystery of marriage without Him.

Saving Your Second Marriage
by Les and Leslie Parrott

Sixty percent of second marriages fail. Yours can be among the ones that succeed. Relationship experts Les and Leslie Parrott show you how to beat the odds with flying colors and make remarriage the best thing that's ever happened to you.

we fight too

a conflict survival guide

Introduction

> **Conflict is common to all marriages.**

> **The goal of marriage is not to be conflict-free but to handle conflict correctly when it occurs.**

> **Healthy conflict resolution occurs when couples are willing to seek and grant forgiveness.**

i Where does conflict come from?

What causes quarrels and what causes fights among you? Is it not this, that your passions are at war within you? You desire and do not have, so you murder. You covet and cannot obtain, so you fight and quarrel.

—James 4:1-2

A. Conflict occurs when our desires are not fulfilled— when we don't get what we want.

● Our "rights" have been violated.

● Our expectations have not been met.

● We have been hurt.

B. Our unfulfilled desires may result in _____.

> *Forgiveness is the oil of relationships.*
>
> —Josh McDowell

> > > > > > > > > > > > >

We all have areas where we are most susceptible to anger; areas that "push our buttons."
Check any that you feel apply to you:

○ last minute changes   ○ a stubborn person

○ feeling neglected   ○ unmet desires

○ feeling disrespected   ○ when my children disobey

○ stress in the workplace   ○ yelling

○ unrealistic expectations   ○ feeling my "rights"

○ hurtful words   have been violated

... for the anger of man does not produce the
righteousness that God requires.

—James 1:20

C. Our unfulfilled desires lead to fighting and quarreling.

D. For conflict to be resolved, both husband and wife
must be committed to oneness.

ii Resolving conflict requires
loving confrontation.

A. Before you confront, examine the offense.

1. Determine if the offense requires confrontation.

Good sense makes one slow to anger, and it is his
glory to overlook an offense.

—Proverbs 19:11

○ ○ ○ ○ ○

2. Consider your contribution to the conflict.

- What role did I play?

- What pattern or habit of mine contributed to the conflict?

3. Examine your _____.
   Are you trying to:

- Retaliate?

- Restore?

- Punish?

- Pursue peace?

Remember, your mate is not your enemy.

B. Lovingly confront.

Rather, speaking the truth in love, we are to grow up in every way into him who is the head, into Christ ...

—Ephesians 4:15

1. Speak the truth in _____.

Let no corrupting talk come out of your mouths, but only such as is good for building up, as fits the occasion, that it may give grace to those who hear.

—Ephesians 4:29

2. Approach confrontation carefully.

- Make sure the timing is right.

- Make sure your focus is right.

focus on:	rather than:
one issue	many issues
the problem	the person
behavior	character
specifics	generalizations
facts	judgment of motive
"I" statements	"you" statements
understanding	who's winning or losing

3. Choose your _____ carefully.

    a. Confront with humility.

    b. Speak the truth in love.

4. Your goal is to restore oneness in your marriage.

Brothers, if anyone is caught in any transgression, you who are spiritual should restore him in a spirit of gentleness. Keep watch on yourself, lest you too be tempted.

—Galatians 6:1

Resolving conflict requires forgiveness.

Be kind to one another, tenderhearted, forgiving one another,
as God in Christ forgave you.

—Ephesians 4:32

A. The Bible teaches that all Christians are responsible to God to seek and grant forgiveness.

B. The offender needs to seek forgiveness.

　　1. Begin by admitting to God and to yourself that you were _____.

　　　　● Be specific.

　　　　● Be willing to accept responsibility for the consequences.

　　　　● Consider and be willing to address the attitudes and desires that may have led to the offense.

　　2. _____ seek forgiveness.

seeking forgiveness ‹ ‹ ‹ ‹ ‹

1. Be willing to say you were wrong:
"I was wrong. I shouldn't have _____."

2. Be willing to say you are sorry:
"I am sorry I did _____ and that I caused you to feel _____."

3. Be willing to repent:
"I know that I have hurt you deeply, and I do not wish to hurt you this way again."

4. Be willing to ask for forgiveness:
"Will you forgive me for doing _____?"

C. The offended spouse needs to _____ forgiveness.

1. True forgiveness is not:

   ● Pretending that something did not happen

   ● Conditional

   ● Forgetting

   ● An automatic cure for the hurt

2. Granting forgiveness is:

   ● A choice to set your spouse free from the debt of their offense

   ● An attitude of letting go of resentment and vengeance

   ● The first step toward rebuilding trust

   ● An act of obedience to God

〉〉〉〉〉

granting forgiveness

1. **Do it privately first:**
   "God, I forgive _____ for hurting me."

2. **Do it specifically:**
   "I forgive you for _____."

3. **Do it generously:**
   "Let's settle this issue and get on with building our relationship."

4. **Do it graciously:**
   "I know I've done things like that myself."

D. Begin the process of rebuilding trust.

1. Trust is not automatically reinstated when forgiveness is sought and granted.

2. Trust is rebuilt through consistent behavior over time.

3. Your spouse's hurt does not instantly disappear. Give grace and time.

4. Ask God for patience.

 We minimize conflict when we actively choose to bless one another in marriage.

A. Blessing your spouse begins by cultivating a new attitude.

To sum up, all of you be harmonious, sympathetic, brotherly, kindhearted, and humble in spirit; ...

—1 Peter 3:8 NASB

B. It involves choosing to give a blessing instead of an insult.

... not returning evil for evil or insult for insult, but giving a blessing instead; for you were called for the very purpose that you might inherit a blessing.

—1 Peter 3:9 NASB

1. You choose to respond _____
   when offended.

2. Your focus is on God and the promises of
   His Word.

3. This choice can only be done in the power
   God provides.

C. Blessing your spouse follows the example of Jesus.

1. Refrain your tongue from speaking evil.

〉〉〉〉〉〉   *"Whoever desires to love life and see good days, let him **keep his tongue from evil** and his lips from speaking deceit; ..."*

—I Peter 3:10

2. Turn away from evil.

〉〉〉〉〉〉   *"let him **turn away from evil** ..."*

—I Peter 3:11

3. Do good.

〉〉〉〉〉〉   *"and **do good;** ..."*

—I Peter 3:11

4. Seek to be a _____ ,
not a troublemaker.

"... let him **seek peace** and pursue it. For the eyes of the Lord are on the
righteous, and his ears are open to their prayer. But the face of
the Lord is against those who do evil."

〈 〈 〈 〈 〈 〈

—1 Peter 3:11b-12

*And while being reviled, He [Jesus] did not revile
in return; while suffering, He uttered no threats,
but kept entrusting Himself to Him who judges
righteously.*

—1 Peter 2:23 NASB

review ‹‹‹‹‹ ›››››preview

O Conflict is common in
marriage; learning to
handle conflict correctly
is the goal.

O We can choose to
respond to hurt and
insult with blessing.

O Resolving conflict is
essential to achieving
oneness in marriage.

O Oneness in marriage is
necessary to enjoy
a healthy sexual
relationship.

HomeBuilders Couples Series® Overview

Key Benefits of the HomeBuilders Couples Series:

1. Doesn't require an "expert" Bible teacher, just a facilitator.

2. Requires a short-term commitment.

3. Requires no preparation for the actual study.

4. Emphasizes practical application by completing the HomeBuilders project.

5. Versatile in various situations: small groups, Sunday school classes, neighborhood outreaches, and weekend retreats.

HomeBuilders Tips

1. Your role as a "facilitator" is to encourage others in the group to think and discover what Scripture says, help the group members feel comfortable, and keep things moving forward. The facilitator is to provide an open, warm environment where couples accept one another. Facilitators will also want to review the Leader's Notes before each session.

2. The ground rules for HomeBuilders group members:

   ● Share nothing that will embarrass your spouse.

   ● You may pass on any question.

   ● Complete the project with your spouse prior to each session.

   ● Confidentiality—anything shared stays in the group.

3. It is important to begin the group and end the sessions on time. Also, it is important for couples to make a commitment to attend all the sessions and complete each of the HomeBuilders projects.

proceed to the application project on page 94

application project

a conflict survival guide

This project is adapted from the HomeBuilders Couples Series study *Resolving Conflict in Your Marriage* by Bob and Jan Horner.

warm-up (10 minutes)

To err is human, to forgive divine. —Alexander Pope

Choose one of the following questions to answer and relate to the group:

When you were a child, who taught you the most about what forgiveness is? How did this person teach you?

From your childhood, when was a time you especially remember having to say "I'm sorry"?

Other than Jesus Christ, whom do you look to as an example of a forgiving person? Why?

blueprints (15 minutes)

1. Forgiveness has been defined as "giving up the right to punish another person." Why is this hard to do?

2. Generally speaking, do you find it easier to ask someone for forgiveness or to grant forgiveness to another person? Explain.

3. Read what Jesus says concerning forgiveness in the following verses. From each verse, identify what you find to be important.

"For if you forgive others their trespasses, your heavenly Father will also forgive you, but if you do not forgive others their trespasses, neither will your Father forgive your trespasses."

—Matthew 6:14-15

Then Peter came up and said to him, "Lord, how often will my brother sin against me, and I forgive him? As many as seven times?" Jesus said to him, "I do not say to you seven times, but seventy times seven."

—Matthew 18:21-22

> **HomeBuilders Principle:**
>
> *To maintain a healthy marriage relationship, you must forgive your spouse as God has forgiven you.*

Individually complete the following:

1. Think of an area in your marriage that generates regular conflict. To assist you we have listed five areas of frequent conflict. You may choose one of these or any other which applies.

○ finance   ○ intimacy

○ children   ○ in-laws

○ roles and responsibilities

2. In this area of conflict what behavior(s) does your spouse most frequently exhibit? Check all that apply.

○ refuse to attempt change   ○ shout

○ embrace sinful behaviors   ○ complain

○ make demands   ○ shut down

○ act insensitively   ○ punish my spouse

○ move to excesses   ○ harass

○ passive-aggressive behavior   ○ other:_____

In this area of conflict what behavior(s) do you most frequently exhibit? Check all that apply.

○ refuse to attempt change   ○ shout

○ embrace sinful behaviors   ○ complain

○ make demands   ○ shut down

○ act insensitively   ○ punish my spouse

○ move to excesses   ○ harass

○ passive-aggressive behavior   ○ other:_____

Together with your spouse:

1. Tell your spouse the area you chose as one which generates frequent conflict in your marriage.

2. Pray together, thanking God for

   a. how He has forgiven you and

   b. the gift He has given you in your spouse.

> congratulations! you finished your third project.

resources to the rescue

Fight Fair!
by Tim and Joy Downs

Discover the difference between attacks that hurt and tactics that heal, and learn how to use conflict to build intimacy, and more. Find out how to win at conflict without losing at love!

Peacemaking for Families
by Ken Sande

We all long for a home that is a haven from a world riddled by conflict, but even in the family, conflict is inevitable. Learn to be peacemakers and help guard your family from destructive conflict, deepen your love and intimacy with your spouse, and provide your children with a solid foundation for life.

Choosing Forgiveness
by Nancy Leigh DeMoss

Forgiving like God is a choice that frees us from the burdens of bitterness, anger, and isolation. If you struggle with long-held hurts, God's truth and Nancy's wisdom hold help and healing for you.

also available in audio

marriage after dark
intimacy from God's perspective

>>>>>> sexual intimacy between husband and wife is a reflection of a couple's oneness.

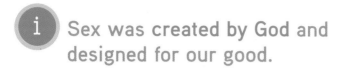 **Sex was created by God and designed for our good.**

A. Sex was meant to be _____ only in the context of marriage.

B. Sex is a gift from God and intended for mutual pleasure.

C. Sex is the divine process for implementing God's command to multiply a godly legacy.

D. Companionship, commitment, passion, and spiritual intimacy are the necessary _____ for a vibrant sexual relationship.

> *Sex is a conversation carried out by other means. If you get on well out of bed, half the problems of bed are solved.*
>
> —Peter Ustinov

100

> > > ## the husband has the freedom to enjoy his wife's body.

"How beautiful are your feet in sandals, O prince's daughter! The curves of your hips are like jewels, the work of the hands of an artist. Your navel is like a round goblet which never lacks mixed wine; your belly is like a heap of wheat fenced about with lilies. Your two breasts are like two fawns, twins of a gazelle. Your neck is like a tower of ivory, your eyes like the pools in Heshbon by the gate of Bath-rabbim; your nose is like the tower of Lebanon, which faces toward Damascus. Your head crowns you like Carmel, and the flowing locks of your head are like purple threads; the king is captivated by your tresses. How beautiful and how delightful you are, my love, with all your charms! Your stature is like a palm tree, and your breasts are like its clusters. I said, 'I will climb the palm tree, I will take hold of its fruit stalks.' Oh, may your breasts be like clusters of the vine, and the fragrance of your breath like apples, and your mouth like the best wine!"

—Song of Solomon 7:1-9 NASB

> > > ## the wife has the freedom to enjoy her husband's body.

"My beloved is dazzling and ruddy, outstanding among ten thousand. His head is like gold, pure gold; his locks are like clusters of dates and black as a raven. His eyes are like doves beside streams of water, bathed in milk, and reposed in their setting. His cheeks are like a bed of balsam, banks of sweet-scented herbs; his lips are lilies dripping with liquid myrrh. His hands are rods of gold set with beryl; his abdomen is carved ivory inlaid with sapphires. His legs are pillars of alabaster set on pedestals of pure gold; his appearance is like Lebanon choice as the cedars. His mouth is full of sweetness and he is wholly desirable. This is my beloved and this is my friend, O daughters of Jerusalem."

—Song of Solomon 5:10-16 NASB

ii Sex is a thermometer that can measure your individual well-being.

A. Sex can be affected by your_____
condition.

- Fatigue
- Diet
- Exercise
- Pregnancy
- Dysfunction

B. Sex can be affected by your

_____

well-being.

- Stress
- Preoccupation
- Incorrect information

C. Sex can be affected by your

_____

health.

- Abuse
- Anger
- Real or false guilt
- Self-perception
- Secrets

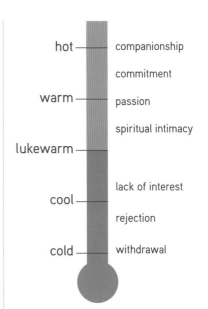

hot —— companionship

commitment

warm —— passion

spiritual intimacy

lukewarm ——

lack of interest

cool ——

rejection

cold —— withdrawal

D. Sex can be affected by your _____ condition.

● Unconfessed sin

● Pornography and romantic fantasies

● Spiritual dryness

● Unreconciled relationships

> making it personal

Check the area that most affects your marital intimacy.

○ your physical condition   ○ your mental well-being

○ your emotional health   ○ your spiritual condition

iii **Sex in marriage can be enhanced by understanding the differences between man and women.**

men		women
physical compartmentalized	**attitude**	relational wholistic
body-centered sight fragrance actions	**stimulation**	person-centered touch attitudes words
respect to be physically needed physical expression	**needs**	security to be emotionally needed intimacy
acyclical quick excitement difficult to distract	**sexual response**	cyclical slower excitement easily distracted
shorter, more intense more physically oriented	**orgasm**	longer, more in-depth more emotionally oriented

 A satisfying sex life is built on a foundation of ...

companionship

communication	tenderness	spending time together
share openly	give creative expressions of affection	share mutual interests
listen carefully	show your love through non-sexual touch	revive the lost art of dating

when companionship is lacking, sex often loses its depth.

commitment

faithfulness	respect	forgiveness
regularly reaffirm your commitment	be a good listener	keep short accounts with each other
build or rebuild trust	validate each other's perspectives and opinions	choose to live in the power of blessing
develop a healthy attitude toward your spouse	never condescend or talk down to each other	remember: "love covers a multitude of sins"
develop a heathly attitude toward sex		

when commitment is lacking, sex can seem risky and can leave a spouse feeling vunerable.

passion

planning	creativity
make it a priority	enhance the setting
schedule it for the best part of your day	vary the approach

when passion is lacking, sex can become routine and stale.

spiritual intimacy

prayer	the Bible
pray together as a couple	spend time reading the Bible together
pray for each other regularly	find verses or passages you can memorize together

when spiritual intimacy is lacking, sex can become shallow and self-focused.

review <<<<<<

- Our pursuit is for a oneness marriage, not just a sexually gratifying relationship.

- A satisfying sex life is the result of a satisfying marriage relationship.

>>>>> preview

- God has given husbands and wives different roles. The better we understand these roles, the better equipped we are to fulfill them.

application project

This application project has two sections: the **individual section** and the **interaction section**. Be sure to leave adequate time to interact as a couple on the interaction section.

Are you remarried?

YES. Then turn to the project on page 112.

individual section

Setting: Stay together as a couple, but complete this section without any interaction.

Objective: To reflect personally on your attitudes toward sexual intimacy and to evaluate the health of your companionship, commitment, passion, and spiritual intimacy.

Instructions: Complete this section individuall..

my attitude toward sexual intimacy

The following questions are for self-reflection and not necessarily intended for sharing in the interaction section. Answer with honesty; there is no requirement that you share this section.

1. When you entered your marriage, what was your perspective on sex and sexual intimacy? ... thoughts? ... fears? ... misconceptions? ... wrong expectations?

2. What problems are these perspectives currently creating
in your sexual relationship?

Thoughts:

Fears:

Misconceptions:

Wrong expectations:

Circle the one that causes the most problems in your relationship.

3. How do you approach problem solving between you
and your spouse in the area of sexual intimacy?
(check all that apply)

○ By trying to fix your spouse

○ By talking together about how to address
your problems

○ By trying to fix yourself

○ By blaming other factors

○ By seeking help or counsel from others (friends,
a pastor, a counselor)

○ By avoiding the subject

○ By finding books, articles, or resources to
provide help

○ By responding in anger

Circle the one you use most often.

4. True or False: The way your spouse looks impacts your attitude toward sexual intimacy. Explain.

5. True or False: Due to the condition of your sexual intimacy, you've pursued sexual fulfillment in other places. Explain.

6. If you answered true to question five, in what ways have these pursuits impacted your marriage?

my satisfaction with our sexual intimacy

How satisfied are you with the way you and your spouse handle the following aspects of your sexual relationship?
> Circle from 1 (low satisfaction) to 5 (high satisfaction) the number that best corresponds to your answer.
> Underline the answer you think your spouse will select.

The quality of our companionship	1	2	3	4	5
The level of our commitment	1	2	3	4	5
The fire of our passion	1	2	3	4	5
The depth of our spiritual intimacy	1	2	3	4	5
Viewing sex with positive anticipation	1	2	3	4	5
The way we decide to have sex together	1	2	3	4	5
The frequency of our physical intimacy	1	2	3	4	5
Gentleness and tenderness during lovemaking	1	2	3	4	5
The variety of our sexual experiences together	1	2	3	4	5
The selflessness displayed in our lovemaking	1	2	3	4	5
The understanding I have of my spouse in this area	1	2	3	4	5
The overall temperature of our love for one another	1	2	3	4	5
The amount of communication during lovemaking (such as discussing better ways of pleasing each other)	1	2	3	4	5

Complete the following as though talking to your spouse:

1. When we make love, the areas you excel in are ...

2. I would enjoy lovemaking even more if you would ...

my relationship with God and our sexual intimacy

1. Realizing that your spouse is a gift from God, in what ways have you rejected or criticized His gift as it relates to sexual intimacy?

2. In personal prayer, confess to God any resentment or bitterness you have toward Him or toward your spouse regarding your sexual relationship.

3. In personal prayer, pray for your spouse and for your sexual relationship together.

interaction section

Setting: Get together with your spouse and complete this section. Make sure you can talk freely.

Objective: To discuss the feelings, attitudes, and thoughts that each of you have on this subject.

Instructions: Interact with an attitude of grace and understanding.

1. Share and discuss any work you completed in the individual section that you are comfortable sharing.

2. Pray together, thanking God for each other. Ask Him to give you greater understanding of each other and a deeper intimacy in your sexual relationship.

> congratulations! you finished your fourth project.

resources to the rescue

Sexual Intimacy in Marriage
by Dr. William Cutrer and Sandra Glahn

This book cuts through the fog of misinformation and partial truths about sex and helps married couples find the fulfillment God intended for the sexual relationship. Perfect for nearly weds, newlyweds, or couples who have been married for years.

Love and Respect
by Emerson Eggerichs

A wife has one driving need—to feel loved. A husband has one driving need—to feel respected. When either of these needs isn't met, things get crazy. *Love and Respect* reveals why spouses react negatively to each other and how they can deal with such conflict quickly, easily, and biblically. 🎧 *also available in audio*

remarried application project

This application project has two sections: the **individual section** and the **interaction section**. Be sure to leave adequate time to interact as a couple on the interaction section.

Are you remarried?

NO. Then turn back to the project on page 106.

individual section

Setting: Stay together as a couple, but complete this section without any interaction.

Objective: To reflect personally on your attitudes toward sexual intimacy and to evaluate the health of your companionship, commitment, passion, and spiritual intimacy.

Instructions: Complete this section individually.

my attitude toward sexual intimacy

The following questions are for self-reflection and not necessarily intended for sharing in the couple section. Answer with honesty; there is no requirement that you share this section.

1. When you entered your marriage, what was your perspective on sex and sexual intimacy? ... thoughts? ... fears? ... misconceptions? ... wrong expectations? In what ways do you think your sexual relationship in your previous marriage has affected your current sexual relationship? What would your spouse say?

2. What problems are these perspectives currently creating in your sexual relationship?

Thoughts:

Fears:

Misconceptions:

Wrong expectations:

The sexual relationship from my previous marriage:

Circle the one that causes the most problems in your relationship.

3. How do you approach problem solving between you and your spouse in the area of sexual intimacy? (check all that apply)

- ○ By trying to fix your spouse
- ○ By talking together about how to address your problems
- ○ By trying to fix yourself
- ○ By blaming other factors
- ○ By seeking help or counsel from others (friends, a pastor, a counselor)
- ○ By avoiding the subject
- ○ By finding books, articles, or resources to provide help
- ○ By responding in anger

Circle the one you use most often.

4. True or False: The way your spouse looks impacts your attitude toward sexual intimacy. Explain.

5. True or False: The issue of comparison regarding sex in your marriage has had a negative impact on your marriage. Explain.

6. True or False: Due to the condition of your sexual intimacy, you've pursued sexual fulfillment in other places. Explain.

7. If you answered true to question six, in what ways have these pursuits impacted your marriage?

my satisfaction with our sexual intimacy

How satisfied are you with the way you and your spouse handle the following aspects of your sexual relationship?

> Circle from 1 (low satisfaction) to 5 (high satisfaction) the number that best corresponds to your answer.
> Underline the answer you think your spouse will select.

The quality of our companionship	1	2	3	4	5
The level of our commitment	1	2	3	4	5
The fire of our passion	1	2	3	4	5
The depth of our spiritual intimacy	1	2	3	4	5
Viewing sex with positive anticipation	1	2	3	4	5
The way we decide to have sex together	1	2	3	4	5
The frequency of our physical intimacy	1	2	3	4	5
Gentleness and tenderness during lovemaking	1	2	3	4	5
The variety of our sexual experiences together	1	2	3	4	5
The selflessness displayed in our lovemaking	1	2	3	4	5
The understanding I have of my spouse in this area	1	2	3	4	5
The overall temperature of our love for one another	1	2	3	4	5
The amount of communication during lovemaking (such as discussing better ways of pleasing each other)	1	2	3	4	5

Complete the following as though talking to your spouse:

1. When we make love, the areas you excel in are ...

2. I would enjoy lovemaking even more if you would ...

my relationship with God and our sexual intimacy

1. Realizing that your spouse is a gift from God, in what ways have you rejected or criticized His gift as it relates to sexual intimacy?

2. In personal prayer, confess to God any resentment or bitterness you have toward Him or toward your spouse regarding your sexual relationship.

3. In personal prayer, pray for your spouse and for your sexual relationship together.

interaction section

Setting: Get together with your spouse and complete this section. Make sure you can talk freely.

Objective: To discuss the feelings, attitudes, and thoughts that each of you have on this subject.

Instructions: Interact with an attitude of grace and understanding.

1. Share and discuss any work you completed in the individual section that you are comfortable sharing.

2. Pray together, thanking God for each other. Ask Him to give you greater understanding of each other and a deeper intimacy in your sexual relationship.

> congratulations! you finished your fourth project.

resources to the rescue

Sexual Intimacy in Marriage
by Dr. William Cutrer and Sandra Glahn

This book cuts through the fog of misinformation and partial truths about sex and helps married couples find the fulfillment God intended for the sexual relationship. Perfect for nearly weds, newlyweds, or couples who have been married for years.

Love and Respect
by Emerson Eggerichs

A wife has one driving need—to feel loved. A husband has one driving need—to feel respected. When either of these needs isn't met, things get crazy. *Love and Respect* reveals why spouses react negatively to each other and how they can deal with such conflict quickly, easily, and biblically. *also available in audio*

woman to woman

embracing God's wonderful design

> *The fact that I am a woman does not make me a different kind of Christian, but the fact that I am a Christian does make me a different kind of a woman. For I have accepted God's idea of me, and my whole life is an offering back to Him of all that I am, and all that He wants me to be.*
>
> —Elisabeth Elliot
> *Let Me Be a Woman*

>>>>>> a wise woman embraces God's design for her home.

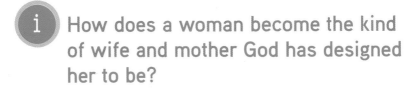

ⓘ **How does a woman become the kind of wife and mother God has designed her to be?**

A. She orders her life according to God's priorities.

   1. Growing in her relationship with God comes first.

   2. Respecting and supporting her husband comes second.

   3. Teaching and training her children come third.

B. She orders everything else in her life (outside activities, job and career, volunteer work, etc.) around these top three priorities.

A discerning woman chooses God's design rather than yielding to other influences.

A. She intentionally pursues a relationship with God.

1. She spends time regularly praying and reading her Bible.

2. She is actively involved in a local church that teaches the Bible.

3. She takes advantage of opportunities to better understand what the Bible teaches.

4. She spends time with other women who share her faith in God.

B. She welcomes God's design for her marriage.

1. God created the man to be the _____ in marriage.

2. God created the woman to be man's helper and completer in marriage.

Then the Lord God said, "It is not good that the man should be alone; I will make him a helper fit for him."

—Genesis 2:18

● "Helper" is a title of worth.

● God refers to Himself in Scripture as our helper.

Behold, God is my helper; the Lord is the upholder of my life.

—Psalm 54:4

121

3. Husbands and wives have equal value but different roles, responsibilities, and purposes.

There is neither Jew nor Greek, there is neither slave nor free, there is no male and female, for you are all one in Christ Jesus.

—Galatians 3:28

C. She actively works at being the best wife she can be.

A wise woman builds her house, but the foolish tears it down with her own hands.

—Proverbs 14:1

1. Her marriage is her most important human relationship.

2. This relationship takes priority over her relationship with her children, other family members, and friends.

D. She gives significant daily attention to her responsibility and call as a mother.

〈 〈 〈 〈 〈 〈 〈 〈 〈 〈

1. A woman's home is the place from which she can change the _____.

2. Building young men and women for the next generation is a most noble task.

> *The mother is the one supreme asset of the national life. She is more important, by far, than the successful statesman, or businessman, or artist, or scientist.*
>
> —Theodore Roosevelt

〉 〉 〉 〉 〉 〉 〉 〉 〉 〉 biblical priorities are at the heart of becoming the wife and mother God intends us to be.

(iii) A strong woman demonstrates love for her husband by respecting and supporting him.

... let the wife see that she respects her husband.

—Ephesians 5:33b

A. Every man has a longing and desire for his wife's respect and support.

B. Respect is a choice to receive your husband in spite of his weaknesses.

This choice _____ your husband to become the man God created him to be.

C. Communicating respect involves your attitude, your words, and your actions.

1. What kind of attitude is necessary?

    a. An attitude of _____respect

> > > > > > God commands wives to respect their husbands without conditions, without his earning it. He is God's gift to you and comes with God's blessing.

    b. An attitude of honor

> > > > > > Respect your husband's authority as the head of the home in front of your children by not challenging him in their presence.

2. What kinds of words are necessary?

a. Words of gratitude

Tell your husband you are grateful for his work to provide for you and the family. His job and career are very important to him. Speak words of thankfulness for all he does.

b. Words of _____

Tell your husband you are proud of him for every choice he makes for good over evil, right over wrong, God's way over his own selfish way.

c. Words of silence

Never criticize or correct your husband in public or in front of the children. You are not his mother.

3. What kinds of actions are necessary?

a. Listening well

Listen to your husband's stories from work as closely as you desire him to listen to you talk of your daily tasks, your life with the children, or your job.

b. Affirming his masculinity by accepting and responding to his sexuality.

Accept and respond to his sexuality. Sexual intimacy is also very important to him. Be consistently seeking to grow in this area of your marriage.

D. Support is a choice to follow your husband's leadership. It empowers him to be all that God intends him to be.

1. The Bible calls following his leadership *submission*.

   Wives, submit to your own husbands, as to the Lord. For the husband is the head of the wife even as Christ is the head of the church ...

   —Ephesians 5:22-23

> Submission *is the divine calling of a wife to honor and affirm her husband's leadership and help carry it through according to her gifts. It's the disposition to follow a husband's authority and an inclination to yield to his leadership. It is an attitude that says,* "I delight for you to take the initiative in our family. I am glad when you take responsibility for things and lead with love. I don't flourish in the relationship when you are passive and I have to make sure the family works."
>
> —John Piper
>
> ©Desiring God. Website: desiringGod.org

2. Submission is a complementary, not competitive, way of _____ to your husband.

   a. Submission does not mean:

   - You are inferior or lose your identity.

   - You blindly obey or submit to verbal or physical abuse.

   - You follow your husband into sin.

    b. Submission does mean:

      ● Giving up your desire to control.

      ● Cooperating with him as he seeks to lead your marriage and family.

E. Demonstrating support or submission also involves your _____, your words, and your actions.

    1. What does a supportive attitude look like?

      a. It is an attitude of trust.

A supportive wife trusts her husband to make decisions even if they are sometimes wrong (from your perspective) trusting that God can correct him and change him.

      b. It is an attitude of faith.

A supportive wife has faith that God is in control of her life, her marriage, her children, her present circumstances, and her future.

Faith is the refusal to panic.
—D. Martin Lloyd Jones

2. What are supportive words that inspire his

_____?

    a. Words of belief

> > > > > >   Believe that God is in control of your life, your marriage, your children, your present circumstances, and your future.

    b. Words of help

> > > > > >   Offer your insights, opinions and feelings on all aspects of your marriage and family (in a respectful way) while communicating that you will follow whatever he ultimately decides. And when you aren't respectful, be sure you apologize afterwards.

    c. Words of affirmation

> > > > > >   Let him know you know that God has called him to lead your home. It will affirm your support and remind him of his responsibility.

3. What are supportive actions that communicate your

_____ to him?

    a. Be ready to follow him where God leads him in his job.

    b. Resist the temptation to be critical of your husband if his decision is not what you would have chosen.

F. With his wife's respect and support, a husband becomes more confident.

G. God is calling you to trust Him and follow His plan even though a positive response from your husband is not guaranteed.

〉〉〉〉〉〉〉〉〉〉〉〉〉

making it personal

In light of everything we talked about, rate the statements below by circling a number from 1 (strongly disagree) to 5 (strongly agree):

Our culture's influence has distracted me from my responsibilities as a wife and mother.	1	2	3	4	5
My attitudes and actions toward my husband show him respect.	1	2	3	4	5
My attitudes toward my husband reflect support and confidence in him.	1	2	3	4	5
My attitudes and actions toward my husband show him love.	1	2	3	4	5
My attitudes toward my husband reflect contentment and trust in God.	1	2	3	4	5
My husband knows I admire him.	1	2	3	4	5
I am willing to follow his direction for our home.	1	2	3	4	5
I accept him regardless of his performance.	1	2	3	4	5
I consider him my top priority.	1	2	3	4	5

An effective mother lovingly teaches and trains her children.

A. She looks carefully at the wisdom for parents that God provides in the Bible.

B. She lovingly and intentionally guides and instructs the next generation.

She opens her mouth with wisdom, and the teaching of kindness is on her tongue.

—Proverbs 31:26

1. She introduces them to _____ and helps them understand the Bible.

2. She communicates the family's values and priorities to her children.

3. She models godly womanhood, knowing that her children are always _____.

4. She provides regular instruction, correction, and discipline.

Hear my son, your father's instruction and forsake not your mother's teaching.

—Proverbs 1:8

5. She does not allow her home to become "child-centered."

... a child left to himself brings shame to his mother ... Discipline your son and he will give you rest; he will give delight to your heart.

—Proverbs 29:15b, 17

○ ○ ○ ○ ○

C. She specifically guides her child in four essential areas.

- Identity

- Character

- Relationships

- Purpose

1. A mother helps her child understand his or her

    _____ as a gift from God.

    a. Children are asking the following questions:

Am I loved	*or*	unloved?
Am I a boy	*or*	a girl?
Am I good	*or*	bad?
Am I valuable	*or*	worthless?

    b. Children need to know what makes them
       unique (personality, gifts, abilities, talents).

2. A mother guides the development of her child's

    _____.

    a. Character is built as you affirm positive attitudes
       and right choices.

    b. Character is built as you instruct and correct.

    c. Good character is reinforced through rewards
       and consequences.

rewards include:	consequences include:
praise and affirmation ☺	☹ time out
increased privileges ☺	☹ assigning extra chores
bonus money ☺	☹ spanking (not in anger)*
activity or trip ☺	☹ removing privileges (TV, computer, toys, activities)
celebration ☺	☹ grounding

✱ Read "The Guidelines for Parental Use of Disciplinary Spanking" from the American College of Pediatricians found in appendix b.

3. A mother trains her child in how to establish healthy _____.

Children must be taught to:

a. Honor and respect parents

b. Respond appropriately to people and authority

c. Be unselfish and put others first

Do nothing from rivalry or conceit, but in humility count others more significant than yourselves. Let each of you look not only to his own interests, but also to the interests of others.

—Philippians 2:3-4

d. Be _____, compassionate, and loyal.

○ ○ ○ ○ ○

4. A mother prepares her children for a life of
_____. Children are prepared
as you and your husband help them:

a. Understand their purpose as a child of God

b. Discover their gifts and talents, strengths
and weaknesses

c. See their parents loving and caring for others

d. Participate in serving God and others
(mission trips, serving at church, caring
for those in need, etc.)

D. She helps to shape the future by equipping and
influencing the next generation.

> > > > > > > involvement is at the heart of teaching
and training children.

> > > > > > > > > > > > >

In light of everything we just talked about, rate the statements below by circling a number from 1 (strongly disagree) to 5 (strongly agree):

I communicate love and admiration for my husband in front of our children.

1   2   3   4   5

Biblical priorities are more important to me than status and lifestyle.

1   2   3   4   5

I save time and energy to nurture my children.

1   2   3   4   5

I model the character I want my children to emulate.

1   2   3   4   5

My home (marriage and family) is a top priority.

1   2   3   4   5

I have regular communication with other mothers committed to biblical principles so I will be encouraged and accountable.

1   2   3   4   5

V A wise woman depends on God.

A. Many women are overwhelmed by their responsibilities as a wife and mother. Marriage and parenting are often very hard work.

B. Remember your priorities. Your relationship with God comes first, followed by your support of your husband and your care for your children.

C. The Holy Spirit will empower you to do what may seem impossible.

D. Trust God's design. Follow His plan. Leave the results to Him.

> *Her children rise up and call her blessed; her husband also, and he praises her: "Many women have done excellently, but you surpass them all." Charm is deceitful, and beauty is vain, but a woman who fears the LORD is to be praised.*
>
> —Proverbs 31:28-30

> > > > > > > > will you choose to become the woman God designed you to be?

review ‹‹‹‹‹

- A wife's understanding of her role in her marriage is crucial to oneness with her husband.

- God's power is always available for you to accomplish God's plan for your life.

› › › › › preview

- The best practices of healthy marriages result in oneness.

> > > > > > > > > > > > > > >

making it personal

Think about what you've heard this morning.

What is one thing that stands out—an area where, with God's help, you want to make a change?

Between now and the next session, find a place where you can share with your husband some of what you learned here this morning.

resources to the rescue

For Women Only
by Shaunti Feldhahn

Do you have a hard time understanding why men behave the way they do? Do you ever wish you could get inside the mind of your husband? Discover eye-opening revelations that will help you understand how to love your man for who he is.

also available in audio

Intimate Issues
by Linda Dillow and Lorraine Pintus

This insightful book is biblical, humorous, practical, and honest. Christian wives will find hope, insight, and a variety of ideas to enhance their relationship with the husbands they love.

man to man

stepping up to a higher call

 # A man takes responsibility to follow Christ.

> *I mean to make myself a man, and if I succeed in that, I shall succeed in everything else.*
>
> —James A. Garfield

Be watchful, stand firm in the faith, act like men, be strong. Let all that you do be done in love.

—1 Corinthians 16:13-14

A. He acknowledges Christ as the absolute _____ in his life.

● He follows Christ.

"If anyone would come after me, let him deny himself and take up his cross and follow me."

—Matthew 16:24

● He obeys Christ.

"If you love me, you will keep my commandments."

—John 14:15

● He depends on the Spirit moment to moment.

If we live by the Spirit, let us also walk by the Spirit.

—Galatians 5:25

B. He courageously assumes the responsibility to love and lead his wife and family.

A man takes responsibility for his role as a husband.

A. God has designated the husband as the _____ of the relationship.

For the husband is the head of the wife, as Christ is also the head of the church, He Himself being the Savior of the body.

—Ephesians 5:23 NASB

1. His leadership is not based on superior abilities but on divine placement.

2. Headship means:

   ● Assuming responsibility for the marriage

   ● Being accountable to God

   ● It does not mean being a bully or boss or dictator.

3. God has designed the husband and wife with

   _____ _____.

   There is neither Jew nor Greek, there is neither slave nor free, there is neither male nor female, for you are all one in Christ Jesus.

   —Galatians 3:28

4. A wise husband values his wife as his partner and helper.

   Then the LORD God said, "It is not good that the man should be alone; I will make him a helper fit for him."

   —Genesis 2:18

B. He sacrificially loves his wife.

Husbands, love your wives, as Christ loved the church and gave himself up for her ... In the same way husbands should love their wives as their own bodies. He who loves his wife loves himself. For no one ever hated his own flesh, but nourishes and cherishes it, just as Christ does the church.

—Ephesians 5:25, 28, 29

1. He _____ his wife by:

- Being trustworthy

- Making her load lighter, not heavier

- Listening to her

- Praying with her

- Putting her needs ahead of his own

2. He _____ his wife by:

- Helping her develop and utilize her gifts and abilities

- Helping her fulfill her purpose and dreams

- Showing her and telling her he loves her

- Making romance a priority

Likewise, husbands, live with your wives in an understanding way, showing honor to the woman as the weaker vessel, since they are heirs with you of the grace of life, so that your prayers may not be hindered.

—1 Peter 3:7

C. He courageously leads his wife.

But I want you to understand that the head of every man is Christ, the head of a wife is her husband, and the head of Christ is God.

—1 Corinthians 11:3

1. His leadership includes providing for his wife's needs by:

- Taking the initiative to meet his family's material needs

- Managing the family's finances wisely

- Making sure his wife and children are taken care of first

    But if anyone does not provide for his relatives, and especially for members of his household, he has denied the faith and is worse than an unbeliever.

    —1 Timothy 5:8

2. His leadership includes protecting his wife by:

- Taking the initiative to meet his family's emotional and spiritual needs

- Keeping her safe from physical harm

- Shielding her from destructive relationships

> > > > > > abdicating or abusing your responsibilities as a husband is taken seriously by God.

"... the LORD has been a witness between you and the wife of your youth, against whom you have dealt treacherously, though she is your companion and your wife by covenant. But not one has done so who has a remnant of the Spirit ... Take heed then to your spirit, and let no one deal treacherously against the wife of your youth."

—Malachi 2:14-15 NASB

> If we *abdicate* our responsibilities, we force our wife to learn to live without us.

> If we *abuse* our responsibilities, we force our wife to either run or retaliate.

142

> > > > > > > > > > > > >

making it personal

In light of everything we just talked about, rate the statements below by circling a number from 1 (strongly disagree) to 5 (strongly agree):

The world's plan has distracted me from my responsibilities as a husband and father.	1	2	3	4	5
My leadership style makes biblical submission easy and reasonable for my wife.	1	2	3	4	5
My leadership style makes my wife feel cherished and understood.	1	2	3	4	5
My leadership is characterized by taking the initiative.	1	2	3	4	5
I verbalize acceptance and honor to my wife.	1	2	3	4	5
I show love for my wife with sacrificial action.	1	2	3	4	5
I demonstrate love even when I don't feel it.	1	2	3	4	5
I know my wife's needs.	1	2	3	4	5
I esteem my wife in her role as a wife (and mother).	1	2	3	4	5
I live with my wife in an understanding way.	1	2	3	4	5
I am growing spiritually.	1	2	3	4	5
My wife knows she is my top priority.	1	2	3	4	5

○ ○ ○ ○ ○

 A man takes responsibility for his role as a father.

A. God has given a father the responsibility to prepare his children for _____.

Fathers, do not provoke your children to anger, but bring them up in the discipline and instruction of the Lord.

—Ephesians 6:4

1. He first _____ his children as a gift from God.

  ● He recognizes each child is an individual, not part of a herd.

  ● He spends time getting to know each child's unique design.

  ● He spends one-on-one time with each child on a regular basis.

2. He eventually _____ his children to fulfill God's plan for their lives.

Behold, children are a heritage from the LORD, the fruit of the womb a reward. Like arrows in the hand of a warrior are the children of one's youth.

—Psalm 127:3-4

● He recognizes that his children belong to God, not to him.

● He helps them discover their purpose and pursue their dreams.

● He encourages and affirms God's work in their lives.

B. He sacrificially loves his children.

Shepherd the flock of God that is among you, exercising oversight, not under compulsion, but willingly, as God would have you; not for shameful gain, but eagerly; not domineering over those in your charge, but being examples to the flock.

—1 Peter 5:2-3

1. He demonstrates that he _____ for them.

● He considers it a privilege to care for them—he does it *willingly*.

● He makes his children a priority—he does it *eagerly*.

● He is careful not to over-control his children—he is *not domineering*.

● He is an example—he does it *consistently*.

2. He cultivates his relationship with them.

- He asks them questions about their day and listens to them.

- He regularly hugs them and tells them he loves them.

- He spends time doing things they enjoy doing.

- He prays with them.

C. He courageously leads his children.

By wisdom a house is built, and by understanding it is established; by knowledge the rooms are filled with all precious and pleasant riches.

—Proverbs 24:3-4

1. He leads by example.

- He cultivates godly character (integrity, honesty, compassion, humility, etc.). What a man is determines what a man does.

Do not be conformed to this world, but be transformed by the renewal of your mind, that by testing you may discern what is the will of God, what is good and acceptable and perfect.

—Romans 12:2

- He practices spiritual disciplines (Bible study, prayer, fellowship with other Christians, etc.).

... train yourself for godliness.

—1 Timothy 4:7b

- He loves their mother.

2. He leads by instruction.

*And these words that I command you today
shall be on your heart. You shall teach them
diligently to your children, and shall talk of
them when you sit in your house, and when you
walk by the way, and when you lie down, and
when you rise.*
                                    —Deuteronomy 6:6-7

● He spends age-appropriate time with them
  reading the Bible and in prayer.

*Hear, O sons, a father's instruction, and be
attentive, that you may gain insight, for I
give you good precepts; do not forsake my
teaching.*
                                    —Proverbs 4:1-2

● He takes advantage of informal teaching
  times.

● He provides opportunities for them to grow on
  their own (church, youth group, camp, etc.).

*If any of you lacks wisdom, let him ask
God, who gives generously to all without
reproach, and it will be given him.*
                                    —James 1:5

> **If we *abdicate* our responsibilities as fathers,
  we force our children to learn life from others.**

> **If we *abuse* our responsibilities as fathers,
  we provoke our children to either run away
  or retaliate.**

〉〉〉〉〉〉〉〉〉〉〉〉

making it personal

In light of everything we just talked about, rate the statements below by circling a number from 1 (strongly disagree) to 5 (strongly agree):

I initiate spiritual guidance to my children.	1	2	3	4	5
I model the character I want my children to emulate.	1	2	3	4	5
I use daily opportunities to equip and train my children.	1	2	3	4	5
I am aware of each of my children's unique needs.	1	2	3	4	5
I am spending consistant time studying the Bible so our family remains biblically accurate.	1	2	3	4	5
My children see me demonstrating sacrificial love for their mother.	1	2	3	4	5

Look at your your answers above and review your answers from page 143.

What is one thing that stands out—an area where, with God's help, you want to make a change?

Between now and the next session, find a place where you can share with your wife some of what you learned here this morning.

 A wise man depends on God.

> **A.** Many men feel overwhelmed by their roles as husbands and fathers.

> **B.** God will empower you to do what may seem impossible.

review <<<<< | >>>>> preview

- A man is called by God to love by leading, providing, and protecting his wife and children.

- God's power is available for a man to accomplish these things.

- The best practices of healthy marriages result in oneness.

the voice of a victim

I can't because ...

my Dad ...

I might fail.

my wife won't ...

I don't know how.

I don't have any help or support in the church.

the choice of a victor

I will ...

follow the example of Jesus.

depend upon God's power.

receive my wife as a good gift from God.

obey God's Word.

seek help and support from godly men.

resources to the rescue

Tender Warrior
by Stu Weber

Will the real men please stand up! It's tough being a man, especially in a culture that isn't sure what manhood really means. Become the "tender warrior" that God intended—tender, yet tough; sensitive, yet strong—and revolutionize your life and relationships.

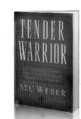

also available in audio

how marriages thrive

essential elements of a oneness marriage

>>>>>>>> a oneness marriage consists of three
essential ingredients.

i Essential #1: the habit of extravagant love

... you yourselves have been taught by God to love one another.

—1 Thessalonians 4:9b

A. Extravagant love _____
the love of God.

B. Extravagant love is:

1. **Exclusive**—One person has your heart for a lifetime.

2. **Expressed**—It is repeated often through words and actions.

3. **Extraordinary**—It places your spouse's needs above your own.

C. Extravagant love is a choice, not a feeling.

D. Extravagant love leads to genuine _____.

> *Success in marriage does not come merely through finding the right mate, but through being the right mate.*
>
> —Barnett R. Brickner

Essential #2: the habit of generous forgiveness

... if one has a complaint against another, forgiving each other; as the Lord has forgiven you, so you also must forgive.

—Colossians 3:13

A. Generous forgiveness begins with humility.

B. Without the habit of generous forgiveness, marriages are filled with _____.

C. Generous forgiveness is:

1. Offered quickly

2. Applied freely

3. Expressed graciously—it keeps no record of wrongs.

D. Generous forgiveness leads to true _____.

> Once a woman has forgiven her man, she must not reheat heat his sins for breakfast.
>
> —Marlene Dietrich

iii Essential #3: the habit of enthusiastic encouragement

Therefore encourage one another and build one another up.

—1 Thessalonians 5:11

> *Often the difference between a successful marriage and a mediocre one consists of leaving about three or four things a day unsaid.*
>
> —Harlan Miller

A. Enthusiastic encouragement believes in and motivates your spouse to grow.

B. Enthusiastic encouragement:

   1. Openly affirms your spouse

   2. Avoids critical words

   3. Maintains a positive attitude, even in hard times

C. Enthusiastic encouragement leads to authentic

   _____.

iv Combining these ingredients leads to a revolutionary relationship.

A. This relationship grows stronger and deeper over time.

B. Extravagant love, generous forgiveness, and enthusiastic encouragement are the ingredients of real oneness.

notes

resources to the rescue

Building Your Mate's Self-Esteem
by Dennis and Barbara Rainey

You can bring out the best in the one you love. The Raineys speak openly and frankly about how to honor, encourage, and build up your mate. Rich in practical insights and anecdotes, this marriage classic addresses the unique issues of today's couple.

Love and Respect
by Emerson Eggerichs

A wife has one driving need—to feel loved. A husband has one driving need—to feel respected. When either of these needs isn't met, things get crazy. *Love and Respect* reveals why spouses react negatively to each other and how they can deal with such conflict quickly, easily, and biblically. *also available in audio*

leaving a legacy
what kind of legacy will you leave?

>>>>>>>> a godly legacy requires more than an inward focus. it requires thinking outwardly as well.

Do not neglect to do good and to share what you have, for such sacrifices are pleasing to God.

—Hebrews 13:16

i **Leaving a godly legacy requires a reality check.**

A. Reality will challenge your commitment to Christ.

B. Reality will challenge your commitment to one another.

C. Facing reality requires persistence.

- Persist through the attacks from Satan, the flesh, and the world.

- Persist through the discouragement caused by lack of immediate results.

- Don't wait for your spouse to act. Do what God expects of you.

What we do for ourselves dies with us. What we do for others and the world remains and is immortal.

—Albert Pine

D. Don't try to do it alone.

- Become an active part of a church that teaches the Bible.

- Find an accountability partner or group. (If you can't find one, start one.)

- Spend time with other couples who can support and encourage you in your marriage.

E. God will honor your faithfulness.

ii Leaving a godly legacy requires developing a godly family.

A. The family is God's smallest battle formation. Make sure your family is equipped for the fight.

1. Identify God's principles that are most strategic.

2. Apply God's principles in the days ahead.

> > > > > > > > > > > > > >

making it personal

Turn to the Take It Home box on page 1 of the manual. Write one, two, or three things you are going to begin doing when you return home.

B. A godly family reaches out to others with the hope of God's Word.

C. What you do today will affect future generations!

iii Leaving a godly legacy requires putting a stake in the ground.

notes

---

resources to the rescue

Growing a Spiritually Strong Family
by Dennis and Barbara Rainey

Do you desire a clear, workable master plan for leading your family to a dynamic faith? The ten brief, yet power-packed chapters are an invitation for you to push aside the distractions that surround you and refocus on what really counts: God, His Word, family, and eternity.

Little House on the Freeway
by Tim Kimmel

Your schedule is hurried and you and your family's commitments are many. Ready for a change of pace? Learn how to put on the brakes and get off the freeway of life altogether. Don't let the temptation to "keep up with the Joneses" keep you from the peace and incredible relationships God created for you.

a way of hope

Seven Steps Toward Breaking the Cycle of Violence in Your Life

Step One: Recognize the need for change.

Step Two: Understand that healthy relationships have boundaries.

Step Three: Seek outside help and guidance.

Step Four: Determine the level of danger and develop a safety plan.

Step Five: Move toward personal recovery by establishing a strong relationship with God.

Step Six: Encourage your husband to get help.

Step Seven: Move toward reconciliation.

Sara's Story

The story on the following pages is true, but details have been changed to protect the woman who tells it.

I was 17 years old, and about to enter my senior year of high school. I met Kurt, a terrific guy who thought I was "perfect," and we started dating. I thought I was in love.

Kurt lived a couple of hours away, so it was a long-distance relationship (I'm sure my parents were thankful). We talked on the phone every Wednesday for an hour or so. Some weekends, my parents would allow him to spend the weekend at our house with strict rules in force. I was always very obedient and knew not to step out of line.

My first indication that he had a temper was during a phone conversation one Wednesday. Kurt and his dad had just had a fight and he told me he had put his fist through his bedroom wall. When I told my mom about this, her comment was, "If he's hitting walls today, he might be hitting you tomorrow." I told her he would never do that because he loved me too much.

We were married three weeks after my high school graduation. My parents were devastated that I was not attending college; it had been their dream and mine for years. I had never had any real confidence in my abilities and practically no self-esteem. So I took the easy way out.

Soon, I noticed that my new husband was extremely jealous and protective. He accused me of sleeping with his friends. He would not allow me to visit my family; he seemed to feel threatened when anyone took attention away from him. When my parents would come into town to visit, he wouldn't allow me to go shopping with my mom or spend time with them. He didn't allow me to go anywhere without him and only he could drive our vehicle.

Even worse, I was becoming afraid of him. He had begun to fly into rages for no apparent reason. Up to this point, the worst that had happened were horrible arguments and lots of tears. Every outburst was followed by flowers and apologies that he wouldn't do it again.

Then I found out I was pregnant. Kurt seemed so happy and anxious. Then within a few months it seemed that all hell broke loose. It started one day as we were driving. He said this child couldn't be his, that he knew I had been with someone else, then he began screaming and calling me names. Then his fist seemed to come out of nowhere—hitting me in the stomach! I remember grabbing my stomach, doubling over, and moaning out loud. I was terrified that he had hurt the baby and I really couldn't believe what had just happened.

Kurt immediately pulled off the road and tried to hug me as his tears flowed. He kept asking me to forgive him, and he promised it would never happen again. I was hurting so bad I just wanted to die.

He kept his word for a few weeks. But then he flew into a rage one night and began throwing things and breaking anything in his path. This continued off and on until our son was born. Then life truly became a living hell.

The rages were even more frequent; now Kurt was convinced that I was sleeping with my coworkers. Nothing I said could convince him that I wasn't. The physical abuse really began at this point. I tried to cover the bruises with makeup or with long sleeves. I was so afraid my coworkers would find out and I couldn't bear the embarrassment.

Kurt began calling me at work to "check up on me." Then he started missing work and sitting in the adjoining parking lot so he could watch my office building. I felt alone and confused. I wanted to tell my parents, but I was afraid they wouldn't understand.

One night we went to the store and were bringing groceries in when something set him off. I was bringing our son in from the car when Kurt attacked me and shoved me down the stairs. I lost my balance and fell backward with Michael in my arms. I was trying to hold onto him with one arm and trying to stop us with the other. Finally, about halfway down, we landed and blood was everywhere. By the grace of God, our son's arm was only scratched, but my leg and knee were gashed.

I told Kurt that I would kill him if he ever laid another hand on me when our son was nearby. Kurt began crying, apologizing, and begging me to forgive him. I was repulsed by what I saw in him and what I saw in myself. I remember crying out to God and asking Him to protect my son and me.

You Are Not Alone

Your story may not sound exactly like the one you just read, but perhaps you can relate in some ways to her experience. When you are abused, you feel desperately alone. You may think, Why me? Other women don't have this problem. Something must be wrong with me. And you may feel so ashamed that this is happening to you that you don't want anyone to know about it. But the truth is that many wives suffer some form of domestic abuse regardless of racial, religious, educational, or economic backgrounds.

According to the American Medical Association, husbands and boyfriends severely assault as many as four million women every year. One in four women will experience some type of spousal abuse during her lifetime.[1] Many of these women feel trapped, anxious, afraid, and helpless. Some feel they are to blame—that if they could just do better at pleasing their husbands, they could change their situations. Others don't know what to do, or where to go to get help. Most suffer in silence, hiding their situations from family and friends because of the shame and embarrassment they feel. Or perhaps they fear others will not believe them.

No, you are not alone. But there is hope! Many women have taken bold and courageous steps to seek help, to find freedom from abuse, and to begin the journey toward a new life. Some have even seen their abusers find the help they desperately needed to stop their destructive behavior and to experience healing and recovery in their own lives. Some couples, through the help of intervention and a structured recovery process guided by pastors or qualified counselors, have been able to experience healing and reconciliation in their marriages.

Yes, it is true that change does take time, a lot of courage, and a great deal of support, but change can happen. And if you are in an abusive situation, change must happen.

What Is Abuse?

A crucial first step in this process will be to acknowledge and understand the abuse occurring in your marriage. Abuse means to mistreat or misuse someone. People abuse others to dominate or control, or to prevent others from making free choices.

There are several different forms of abuse:

- **Emotional or psychological abuse:** Mistreating and controlling someone through fear, manipulation, and intimidation, and by attacking that person's sense of self-worth. The abuser seeks to make his wife feel afraid, helpless, confused, and worthless. This form of abuse includes name-calling, mocking, belittling, accusing, blaming, yelling, swearing, harassing, isolating from family and friends, abusing authority, withholding emotional support and affection, and betraying trust.

- **Physical abuse:** Assaulting, threatening, or restraining a person through force. Men who batter use physical violence to control women—to scare them into doing whatever they want them to do. Physical abuse includes hitting, slapping, punching, beating, grabbing, shoving, biting, kicking, pulling hair, burning, using or threatening the use of weapons, blocking you from leaving a room or the house during an argument, driving recklessly, or intimidating you with threatening gestures.

- **Sexual abuse:** Behavior that dominates or controls someone through sexual acts, demands or insults. Sexual abuse includes making you do sexual things when it is against your will, when you are sick, or when it is painful; using force (including rape in or out of marriage), threats, or coercion to obtain sex or perform sexual acts; forcing you to have unprotected sex, or sex with others; treating you like a sex object, and calling you names like "frigid" or "whore."

Facing the Facts ... and Facing Your Fears

Denying the abuse or the impact of abuse may have helped you to cope with the problem until now. However, denial is also the very thing that will hinder you from breaking the cycle of violence in your life, and from experiencing peace and freedom from abuse. The fact that you are reading this book is evidence that you are willing to acknowledge the abuse. You've already taken a courageous step.

Facing the fact that you are being abused or battered by your husband, and that his behavior is not normal, can stir up deep emotional feelings—especially fear. You must acknowledge these fears in order to face and deal with the problem. In her book, *Invisible Wounds: A Self-Help Guide for Women in Destructive Relationships,* Kay Douglas writes, "Unacknowledged fears play on our minds and sap our confidence until we have no energy left to deal with the problems at hand. The way out of fear is through it." She goes on to say, "As we face and feel our vulnerability, our fear may increase in intensity for a brief time. Then it begins to diminish. When we know what we are dealing with, much of the power of that feeling goes. We move through fear to a calmer, stronger place within. Having faced the worst, we are free to put our energy into coping creatively with our situation."[2]

It's Time to Make the Right Choices

You do not deserve to be abused, nor are you to blame for the abuse that you have suffered. Abuse of any type is wrong, and if you are in an abusive situation, the first step toward new life and freedom is to recognize that there is a need for a change in your life. Change can be difficult, and in some cases, change can be frightening. However, in any type of an abusive situation, change is absolutely necessary for your own well-being.

Remember, abuse is about power and control. You may be experiencing verbal or emotional abuse now. But if changes are not made to resolve your current situation, then when your

husband begins feeling as if he still does not have enough control, the abuse will escalate into more violent forms. According to the Metro Nashville Police Domestic Violence Division, "When abusers hit or break objects or make threats, almost 100 percent resort to physical battering."[3] What might be verbal abuse now could turn into physical abuse down the road. No form of abuse is acceptable!

Contrary to what you may believe, you are not powerless! You are a worthwhile person and you do not have to continue to accept the mistreatment of your husband. You have the power to make your own choices.

Notes:

1. Lou Brown, Francois Dubau, Merritt McKeon, J.D., *Stop Domestic Violence: An Action Plan for Saving Lives* (St. Martin's Griffin, 1997), p. xiii.

2. Kay Douglas, *Invisible Wounds: A Self-Help Guide for Women in Destructive Relationships* (Penguin Books, New Zealand, 1996), p. 176.

3. Quoted by permission from material provided by Metro Nashville Police Department Domestic Violence.

This is an excerpt from *A Way of Hope* by Leslie J. Barner (Little Rock, AR: FamilyLife, 2004). *A Way of Hope* is currently out of print.

disciplinary spanking

"guidelines for parental use of disciplinary spanking"
from the American College of Pediatricians

guidelines for parental use of disciplinary spanking

1. Spanking should be used selectively for clear, deliberate misbehavior, particularly that which arises from a child's persistent defiance of a parent's instruction. It should be used only when the child receives at least as much encouragement and praise for good behavior as correction for problem behavior.

2. Milder forms of discipline, such as verbal correction, extinction, logical and natural consequences, and time-out should be used initially, followed by spanking when noncompliance persists. Spanking has been shown to be an effective method of enforcing time-out with the child who refuses to comply.

3. Only a parent, or in exceptional situations someone else who has an intimate relationship of authority with the child, should administer disciplinary spanking.

4. Spanking should not be administered on impulse or when a parent is out of control. A spanking should always be motivated by love, for the purpose of teaching and correcting, and not for revenge or retaliation.

5. Spanking is inappropriate before 15 months of age and is usually not necessary until after 18 months. It should be less necessary after 6 years and rarely, if ever, used after 10 years of age.

6. After 10 months of age, one slap to the hand of a stubborn crawler or toddler may be necessary to stop serious misbehavior when distraction and removal have failed. This is particularly the case when the forbidden object is immoveable and dangerous, such as a hot oven door or an electrical outlet.

7. Spanking should always be a *planned* action (not a reaction) by the parent and should follow a deliberate procedure.

   ● The child should be *forewarned* of the spanking consequence for designated problem behaviors.

   ● Spanking should always be administered in *private* (bedroom or restroom) to avoid public humiliation or embarrassment.

   ● One or two spanks are administered to the buttocks. This is followed by embracing the child and calmly reviewing the offense and the desired behavior in an effort to reestablish a warm relationship.

8. Spanking should leave only transient redness of the skin and should not cause physical injury.

9. If properly administered spankings are ineffective, other disciplinary responses should be tried again rather than increasing the intensity of spankings. Professional help should be obtained when a satisfactory behavioral response cannot be achieved through the process of discipline.

Visit ACPeds.org to download the complete study,
Corporal Punishment: A Scientific Review of Its Use in Discipline,
from the American College of Pediatricians.

weekend to remember **answer key**

why marriages fail
(sessions 1)

encourages
backgrounds
motivations
expectations
performance
self-destruct
anticipate
respond properly
response
escape
search
self-centered
selfishness
reality
romance

can we talk?
(session 2)

freedom
levels
ongoing
listen
express

unlocking the mystery of marriage
(session 3)

together
oneness
lifetime
Companionship
before
context
multiply
team
Satan
independence
attacks

from how to wow
(session 4)

primary
alone
need
provided
receive
principle
performance
process
couple
differences
hindrances
tools
weaknesses
self-centeredness
needs
receive

what every marriage needs
(session 5)

complete
sin
motivated
relationship
lifelong

we fight too
(session 6)

anger
heart
love
words
wrong
Humbly
grant
kindly
peacemaker

marriage after dark
(session 7)

experienced
ingredients
physical
mental
emotional
spiritual

woman to woman
(session 8)

leader
world
empowers
unconditional
praise
relating
attitude
leadership
loyalty
God
watching
identity
character
relationships
kind
purpose

man to man
(session 8)

leader
head
equal value
cherishes
nourishes
life
receives
releases
cares

how marriages thrive
(session 9)

reflects
intimacy
bitterness
security
unity

leaving a leagcy
(session 10)

(no blanks to fill in)

weekend to remember evaluation

conference city: _____

conference date: _____ date married: _ _ /_ _ /_ _ _ _

last name   first name

name: [ ][ ][ ][ ][ ][ ][ ][ ][ ][ ][ ][ ][ ][ ][ ][ ][ ]   spouse: [ ][ ][ ][ ][ ][ ][ ][ ]

address: [ ]

city: [ ][ ][ ][ ][ ][ ][ ][ ][ ][ ][ ][ ][ ][ ][ ][ ][ ]   state: [ ][ ]   ZIP: [ ][ ][ ][ ][ ]

e-mail address: [ ]

I would like to receive by e-mail: ○ The Family Room   ○ Marriage Memo   ○ HomeBuilders E-News

home phone: ([ ][ ][ ]) [ ][ ][ ][ ][ ][ ][ ]   cell phone: ([ ][ ][ ]) [ ][ ][ ][ ][ ][ ][ ]

age range: ○ 29 or below   ○ 30-39   ○ 40-49   ○ 50-59   ○ 60 or above   ○ male ○ female

if you attend a church, please provide the following information:

church name: [ ]

church city: [ ]

---

you can make a difference

I desire to make a difference in families:

○ I'm interested in bringing a group to a Weekend to Remember.

○ Please contact me about joining the local volunteer team.

life-changing decisions

During this conference, I made the following decision:

○ I received Christ as Lord and Savior.

○ I prayed to be filled with the Holy Spirit.

○ I recommitted my life and family to Christ.

a family partnership

Many of our staff have left their careers to serve as full-time missionaries at FamilyLife. They depend on individuals like you to fund their personal ongoing ministry and living expenses. If you check the box below, one of our staff families will personally contact you about how you can invest financially in their ministry.

○ **Yes, I'd be interested in learning more about financially partnering with a FamilyLife staff member.**

---

1. How would you rate the Weekend to Remember conference?

	poor	fair	good	excellent
overall conference	○	○	○	○
speakers	○	○	○	○
hotel	○	○	○	○
overall value	○	○	○	○

continued on back

2. Did the conference meet your expectations? ○ Yes ○ No   If not, why?

3. Rate the health of your marriage before and after the conference from 1 to 10.

before: unhealthy   1   2   3   4   5   6   7   8   9   10   healthy

after: unhealthy   1   2   3   4   5   6   7   8   9   10   healthy

4. May we contact you in three to twelve months to see how you are doing?
○ Yes ○ No

5. What were the most important things you learned from the conference?

6. What was the highlight of the conference for you?

7. Describe the effect this conference had on you and your spouse.

May we quote you? ○ yes ○ no

8. How did you hear about the Weekend to Remember?

	check all that apply	check only the single most influential
church	○	○
e-mail	○	○
friend/family	○	○
FamilyLife Today broadcast	○	○
radio commercials	○	○
mail	○	○
web site	○	○